GOOD QUESTION!

THE PROFESSIONALS' GUIDE TO CELEBRITY INTERVIEWS

KENNY RHODES

Copyright 2017 © Kenny Rhodes

All rights reserved. No part of this book may be reproduced or transmitted in any form or by any means, electronic or mechanical, including photocopying, recording or by any information storage and retrieval system without written permission of the publisher, except for the inclusion of brief quotations in a review.

ISBN: 978-0-692-96499-6

Cover Design: Clark Fairfield
Illustrations: Russell Frazier
Photos: Daniel Reichert
Interior Design: Christina Gorchos, 3CsBooks.com

DEDICATION

To my wonderful wife Donna and our glorious son Jerome,
the motivation for everything I do.

DEDICATION

FORWARD

When you're doing it right, there are only two people in the world: you and your partner. You're in this together; knee-to-knee in a small, dark room with lights in your eyes, a camera over your shoulder and the "approverrati" hanging on your every word. It's a sobering, nerve-wracking job; and it's a ton of fun.

I'm talking about conducting on-camera, celebrity interviews. I have been doing this for years and had the good fortune to sit down with over three hundred celebrities.[1] I've produced on-air shorts, DVD bonus features and even received an Emmy™ for a TV series I produced based on my interviews. In the course of it all, I've discovered tips, techniques and systems that make

---

[1] See partial list in Acknowledgments.

the process much easier and more enjoyable. This book compiles them all into one place.

When I started out, I would have killed for a roadmap to the journey ahead. A guide would have been invaluable that revealed the shortcuts, detours and speed bumps inherent in this wild ride. I didn't know which questions to ask or what a junket was. I was clueless about how to get past the rote answers and help my partner open up. Surely someone had done this before and written down some rules, right? Well, not so much.

So I had to do it myself, and Good Question! is the result. This book is for the novice who is interviewing a movie star for the first time; the young producer expanding her career; the seasoned professional looking for a refresher on best practices. Whatever your level, the tools in this book will get you started and keep you on track in the years ahead.

I've distilled what I've learned into three sections:

1. **Pre-Production—Preparation**

2. **Production—Conducting the Interview**

3. **Post-Production—Editing**

These sections will provide an overview of the entire interviewing process. I've also included **Checklists** at the end of selected chapters to help you remember the details. And I've described unique tools I call **Key Tips** throughout the book; techniques that I rely upon that consistently yield great results. For your convenience, you can also find these at **GoodQuestionTheBook.com** along with downloadable assets like sample questions, videos, talent releases and other tools to augment the guidelines in these pages.

But I'm getting ahead of myself; let me share a little of my own backstory. I spent my formative years as an actor. I received a BA in Theater Arts from UCLA and made a living working in TV, film and live theatre into my thirties. Then I landed a job as a Production Assistant at FX Networks and rose through the ranks to become a promo writer/producer. I've worked in this arena ever since. Still, due to my background, I will always see the world through the eyes of a performer.

One example of this is my attitude toward *technique*. Every actor hopes for moments of powerful inspiration, when "the muse is upon her" and everything is flowing perfectly like a gift from above. You're in the moment. The problem is the muse is notoriously fickle. You can't count on her showing up and, when she doesn't, you need a set of skills and practices to draw upon. Actors call that technique.

Similarly, some of the most magical moments you will ever experience during an interview happen out of pure luck. Just such a break occurred to me on my very first interview. I was working at an agency in Hollywood when Lifetime TV hired us to create some on-air segments with Meg Ryan, who was starring in the romantic comedy *Kate & Leopold*. We were cautioned, "Be careful; Meg's very smart and doesn't suffer fools gladly." That spooked us a bit, especially as no one in my office had much experience doing celebrity interviews. Knowing my background, however, my boss threw me into the ring. When it was time to meet one of the most famous actresses working, and talk to her about her craft, I gathered my courage and tried to act like I knew what I was doing:

> KR: So, um..., Hi. So. Uh-what's <u>your</u> favorite rom-com? Uh-Romantic. Movie. You know, comedy or otherwise — doesn't have to be —
>
> Meg: Oh, probably *Lawrence of Arabia*.

Didn't see that coming. Luckily *Lawrence* happens to be my favorite film and I practically know it by heart. I quickly re-ran the entire epic in my head and noticed something new:

> KR: Huh. Now that I think of it, there's not a single woman in that entire movie.
>
> MEG: I know, but it's all about the romance of the desert and passion; it just gets me.
>
> KR: [beat] Will you marry me?

No I didn't, but I thought about it. We were now on the same wavelength and, from then on, had a terrific conversation. Unbeknownst to me, I was also on a new career path that led to discussions with fascinating people, thrilling excursions to film festivals, numerous awards and now this book. So, if I haven't said it before, Thanks Meg!

Of course I was lucky that day. But since I can't always count on luck, I've developed techniques to navigate some pretty unpredictable waters. This book outlines those techniques and will get you up to speed quickly. On the other hand, interviewing is an art, and art takes practice. This book also provides skills that you can practice, polish and perfect for as long as you're doing this job.

A few housekeeping items before we get started. First, I refer to my partner throughout this book instead of the interviewee because that's how I feel about the person in the other chair. Together we're collaborating on a creative endeavor and that's the definition of a partner.

Second, I use the pronoun *she* in reference to unknown gender as my small contribution to offset years of male-pronoun-dominated grammar. There, that ought to do it.

Finally, I call this book <u>Good Question!</u> for the simple reason that that's the response I'm always hoping for. When I ask a question, see the light in my partner's eyes and hear those two words, I silently pump the air because I know I've hit pay dirt. It means my preparation has paid off. It signals a bond with my partner. It's unlocks the best information. And it's an incredible thrill that I hope you'll share. Of course, sometimes you'll just get lucky. Until then, you'll want something to fall back on.

Fall back on this book.

TABLE OF CONTENTS

SECTION ONE: PRE-PRODUCTION
THE READINESS IS ALL

CHAPTER ONE
WHAT'S THE ATTRACTION? 1

CHAPTER TWO
YOU CAN'T OVER-PREPARE 7

CHAPTER THREE
CRAFTING GOOD QUESTIONS 21

CHAPTER FOUR
SHORTCUTS AND TRICKS 31

SECTION TWO: PRODUCTION
THE ROOM WHERE IT HAPPENS

PART ONE - AT THE JUNKET 42

CHAPTER FIVE
ARRIVAL 43

CHAPTER SIX
GETTING STARTED 51

CHAPTER SEVEN
IN THE THICK OF IT 59

CHAPTER EIGHT
WRAPPING IT UP AT THE JUNKET 69

PART TWO - IN YOUR OWN HOUSE 74

CHAPTER NINE
SETTING UP YOUR SHOT 79

CHAPTER TEN
CAMERA PLACEMENT 87

CHAPTER ELEVEN
TOPS AND TAILS 97

CHAPTER TWELVE
BEST-LAID PLANS 107

SECTION THREE: POST-PRODUCTION
PUTTING IT TOGETHER

CHAPTER THIRTEEN
PREPPING FOR YOUR EDITOR 115

CHAPTER FOURTEEN
THE THREE-DOCUMENT SYSTEM 121

CHAPTER FIFTEEN
EDITING YOUR INTERVIEW 131

CHAPTER SIXTEEN
MARTINI SHOT 137

ACKNOWLEDGEMENTS 141
ABOUT THE AUTHOR 147

SECTION ONE

 # PRE-PRODUCTION

THE READINESS IS ALL

CHAPTER ONE

WHAT'S THE ATTRACTION?

Conducting a great interview is like riding a spirited horse. A firm but gentle hand on the reins, and a healthy respect for your partner will yield the best results. Your goal is to steer the conversation just enough to get where you're going, but look like you're sitting back and enjoying the ride. That requires confidence, preparation and trust. This book is designed to guide you in that direction.

Throughout this book I will concentrate on a type of interview that is supportive and casual in tone. In this context, your partner and you are on the same side. A combative interrogation has its place, but it's not what I'm here to discuss. I've been fortunate enough to work for clients--network executives and others --who wanted my partner to look and sound her best on-camera, not to trip her up with traps and gotcha questions. This book is designed to give you the skills to draw your partner out in a reassuring, encouraging manner. You will create a safe space for her to reveal specific details about her thoughts and work. If you can pull this off and have fun while you're doing it, you've found the right career.

Interviews are inherently fascinating. The industries that market movies, books, music, fashion, etc. all use interviews to establish their brand and get the word out. It's a format that has stood the test of time because people respond to it viscerally. It's the closest most viewers will ever come to sitting down with newsmakers and celebrities. But it's also much more than that.

Interviews are inherently captivating. There's an old anecdote in live theater that if, during a play, a cat were to wander out onto the stage, no matter how brilliant the performances, the audience would start watching the cat. Simply put: *life before art.* There's an unmistakable energy to authentic, real-time events that always trump the rehearsed. Interviews are that rare combination of both.

I've interviewed some of the giants in the entertainment field, and usually found them to be charming, committed artists who enjoyed discussing their craft. Who wouldn't want to talk to them? Joanne Woodward famously said that, "acting is like sex. You should do it, not talk about it," but actors love to talk about it, and thank goodness for us that they do.

WHO DOES IT BEST?

As in any discipline, this one has its legends and heroes. Here are a few of mine:

- **Bill Maher** – Best known as a stand-up comic and sometime political pundit, his insatiable curiosity has catapulted him to the top of a crowded field. His ability to really listen to people he doesn't always agree with is more than a skill, it's a gift.

- **Ellen DeGeneres** – This icon of daytime television, comedy and activism possesses a unique genius for conducting interviews with humor and candor. Her gentleness and insights make her interviews seem like casual conversations that just happen to touch on deep, funny and intimate subjects.

- **Elvis Costello** – If you've seen his brilliant series, *Spectacle*, you know why he's on this list. With his encyclopedic knowledge of music, no one can touch Elvis (Declan, to his friends) when interviewing fellow musicians. Nothing throws him. Check out the episode with Levon Helm who answered him with drum fills after his voice gave out.

- **Howard Stern** – Shock jock, provocateur, rule breaker. Sure, but he's also a dynamite interviewer. He knows his stuff, he's afraid of nothing, and he attracts the biggest names in entertainment, music and politics because his style is uniquely authentic.

- **Ira Glass** – He has done for non-fiction radio stories what Ken Burns did for documentaries: revitalized the industry with a depth and style that is often copied, but never equaled. His long running NPR show, *This American Life* has helped launch other great interviewers' careers, as well as kept more listeners in their driveways than broken garage door openers.

- **Jerry Seinfeld** – Of course he's hilarious, but he also has some mad skills as an interviewer. If you haven't seen *Comedians In Cars Getting Coffee*, I urge you to treat yourself. No one listens more generously or supports his partner like Jerry Seinfeld. For just one example, don't miss his brilliant job interviewing President Obama.

- **Larry King** – The old lion. You might say he wrote the book on interviews (except he didn't, I checked). He is calm in the face of world leaders, major celebrities and cultural icons and makes the whole process look easy. He achieves this with preparation and direct engagement, and if you can emulate that, you can't go wrong.

- **Oprah Winfrey** – Her accomplishments fill volumes and, as an interviewer alone, she stands among the best. She's always kind, well-informed, and no-nonsense whether her partners are jumping on couches or overcome with grief. Probably her greatest asset, beside her intelligence, is her huge heart that is apparent in every interview. That's a hard thing to emulate, but easy to appreciate.

- **Sacha Baron Cohen** – Don't be surprised to see him on this list. The fertile mind of this British comedian has given birth to characters that take on the world in ways his partners never see coming. He has created a whole new genre of semi-reality comedy as he simultaneously interviews and punks his partners. His interviews may not always be the kindest, but they just might be the funniest. Plus, he kissed me when I interviewed him,[2] so he'll always have a soft spot in my heart.

---

[2] And I can prove it. Check out the clip at GoodQuestionTheBook.com

- **Stephen Colbert** – Talk about making a genre his own! By conducting his interviews in-character, he re-defined reality comedy at the same time he re-envisioned the celebrity interview. Most of his early interviews were with politicians who didn't even know he was putting them on. I will personally never stop thanking him for creating the question format, "George Bush: great president? Or greatest president ever?"

- **Terry Gross** – My personal favorite. No one knows her subject better or puts her partners at ease like Terry. Every interview sounds like she's spent years preparing for it. She's always calm and gracious, and her depth of knowledge and infectious laugh make her interviews sound better than anyone else's, in my humble opinion.

There are dozens of others of course, but these masters hit the important marks that, to me, make a great interviewer. They know their subject incredibly well, they are authentic and they put their partners at ease. Watch the greats and see what you can pick up.

CHAPTER TWO

YOU CAN'T OVER-PREPARE

IT'S JUST A CONVERSATION

Right from the get-go, I urge you to re-frame your expectations: it's not an interview, it's a conversation. You want your partner to feel like she's chatting casually with a friend, not taking a survey. You may have a list of items you need to cover, but if you can hide the artificiality of the job and simply communicate, you're halfway home. Engage her in a casual, authentic discussion. Submerge your agenda--your list of questions--under the guise of informal chit-chat. Start easy. Touch lightly on the subjects you want to cover. Jump around to different topics in a non-linear, unforced way. Let your partner volunteer subjects. Lead her with gentle encouragement until she thinks she's leading you. When you're done, you want to hear her say, "It was great talking to you," and not, "I hope you got what you needed."

The first step toward that goal is preparation. Long before you sit down with your celebrity partner you'll want to plan how you're going to make the most of your limited time. Preparation is your protection against surprises, and research is the key to that preparation. If you hit the marks laid out in this chapter, you'll be ready to get the conversation started.

RESEARCH YOUR PARTNER

Let's face it, celebrities can be intimidating. They're famous, they're glamorous and they're powerful. You've been watching them for years, so you feel like you know them personally, but they don't know you from Adam. And they often come with an entourage that makes them even more formidable.

Yet here's the simple, not very surprising truth: actors are the same as everyone else, just with an additional skill set. Contrary to popular belief, they are not emotionally unbalanced weirdoes that should be quarantined from the wider population lest they pollute the gene pool. In fact, in my experience, they're usually intelligent, generous people who have devoted their time and energy to a well-respected craft that they love. Of course there are some whack jobs, but name an industry where there aren't, I dare you.

Start by finding out whatever you can about your partner. This will not only prepare you for your interview, it will positively affect your presentation, protect you against curveballs and build your confidence. You don't have to be fluent in your partner's life story, just conversant in the high points so you're ready to be an informed interlocutor.

Learning a little trivia doesn't hurt either. I was once talking with an actor who was also a musician. He was discussing his guitar playing when I said, "But you played bass in high school, didn't you?" He paused, smiled and confirmed this with a look that contained a hint of gratitude. This wasn't a secret, but it wasn't especially well-known and I'd gained some respect.

Here's what happens when you don't do the above. I once interviewed Halle Berry for one of the *X-Men* movies and inadvertently broke this rule. I asked her if this was the first time she'd done such a physical part with extensive fights scenes in a big action film. She paused briefly, then very politely mentioned, "Well--no, I did it for the *Bond* movie, and *Cat Woman*, so..." I looked like a clown. She was so gracious that I was able to get on with my interview but I resolved to make sure and avoid that mistake in the future.

It won't matter if you never bring up the trivia you learn about your partner. In the short time you get, there might not be an opportunity. On the other hand, if there's a chance to drop one of your newly learned nuggets, it's a huge point in your favor. Making someone feel that you really *get* her is extremely flattering. Go the extra mile.

USE YOUR RESOURCES

I start with the Internet Movie Database (US.IMDb.com), then move on to anything else I can find. Most stars have their own websites, Facebook pages, fan sites, etc. There is no shortage of information about famous people online so start anywhere and follow wherever it leads. You'll learn a thing or two, and it's good practice for your interview technique, which also benefits from following wherever it leads. Remember to cross-reference what you find, however, as no site is 100% reliable.

Here are a few things I discovered which came in handy during an interview:

- **Kiefer Sutherland fronts a country band.**
- **Thomas Haden Church owns a Texas cattle company.**
- **Richard Gere is a practicing Buddhist and has met the Dalai Lama.**
- **Felicity Huffman's nickname is *Flicka* (which is means *girl* in Swedish).**
- **Meg Ryan was a journalism major at NYU.**

Then, once you know something about her background…

KEY TIP: FIND OUT HOW YOUR PARTNER RESPONDS TO INTERVIEWS.

Google her name and the word *interview* and, if she's even marginally well-known, you'll find interviews she's done in the past. Watch as much as you can to get a sense of how she interacts with interviewers. Is she shy and reserved and needs you to draw her out? Tom Hardy is like that, surprisingly. Is she so gregarious you need to lead her back onto your subject? This is true of Jon Voight. I discovered James Franco could be an incredibly loud talker, but in sudden bursts. He is calm and quiet when he first introduces himself, so this is a quality that occurs when he warms to his subject. I had seen him do it online so I was able to advise my soundman in advance and he was ready to ride the levels of his equipment accordingly. Adam Sandler has a *good side*. Who knew? Well, now I do, and it would have made the studio happier if I'd known sooner. A little research is all it takes.

Then, of course, watch the film or show she's promoting. Duh, right? You'd be amazed at how many people skip this step.

Sometimes there isn't time. Other times it's your preference. Personally I'm not sitting through some torture-porn slasher/zombie flick, no matter who I'm talking to. But you've got to do some homework, so at least read up on your partner's current projects. Watch the trailers. Read the reviews. Scan the fan input. If you're suddenly thrown in with someone you've never heard of and there's no time to prepare – don't bring it up! She will assume you are an expert; let her. In all other cases, get in front of the ball.

Finally--and this is a little dicey--if you haven't seen the work and she asks you directly, lie. Sorry, that's just the best choice. Sometimes you have to fake it, but keep this to a minimum. She won't test you because she'll assume you're prepared. I have seen interviews get shut down because the star discovered that the journalist has not seen her work. Be prepared.

Case in point: I was about to talk to an Oscar-winning actor when he suddenly stormed out of the room right before I went in, leaving a slack-jawed journalist in his wake. He has a reputation for his temper and theatrics so I wrote it off, but later learned the journalist before me admitted to not having seen his film. He felt disrespected. He may have been temperamental, but he wasn't wrong. It took about fifteen minutes before his team could talk him back into the chair, when, of course, it was my turn. Great. Luckily I *had* done my research, and made sure he knew it in the way I phrased my questions--chock full of specifics about the movie.

KEY TIP: ASK THE HANDLERS.

All celebrities are different and the bigger they are, the greater number of folks that manage their image. Whenever possible, talk to these people in advance. Ask to speak with a press agent, manager or anyone who identifies herself as a contact. Your goal is to make your partner as comfortable as possible so find out if there any items you can provide. Does she have a special hair/make-up person that she prefers to work with? Does she favor one side of her face toward camera? Even something as simple as is she hungry or thirsty? One mega-star I won't name surprised us with her answer to our question, "Is there anything we can get you?" with the response, "Vodka, little ice." I won't say if we supplied this social lubricant, I will simply re-state that your partner's comfort is your top priority.

RESEARCH THE VENUE

The next thing to become familiar with is the location in which you'll be conducting the interview. You don't need to go overboard with blueprints or floor plans, but you do need to know what physical opportunities and limitations will be present. The space will dictate the look and feel of your interview. Are you setting up your own shot in an empty hotel room? Are you at an outdoor setting with logistical issues? Or is it a press day that has been set up by a studio, and there's nothing for you to worry about except doing your job?

There are an infinite number of places you could find yourself, but in my experience, they boil down to just two types:

1. **The Junket**
2. **Anywhere else**

In other words, you'll either be the guest of the studio at a junket, or you'll be in a location of your own choosing. Your own shoot gives you the most creative latitude as well as the most responsibility. The press junket streamlines your responsibilities but presents its own unique set of challenges. Let's take a look at that scenario first:

THE JUNKET – AN INTRODUCTION

The junket, or press day as it is also called, serves an incredibly important function for studios and networks. Over the course of one-to-three days, stars and top creatives from movies and TV shows are made available to talk to the press about their work. This provides exclusive content (interview footage) to dozens of different outlets (networks, newspapers, social media) in an incredibly efficient way. The various "talent" stay put while the journalists rotate into each of their rooms, speaking to them in rapid succession. Like celebrity speed-dating.

The upside to the junket is its efficiency. Everything is taken care of for you: The talent is in place. The camera crews have their instructions. The schedules have been worked out and there are back-up plans for contingencies. If you're new to this task, it's a very good place to start because most of the variables have been removed and you can concentrate on your work.

Over the years the format of the junket has changed to suit the needs of the media and the studios, but much of it remains constant. They usually take place in LA, New York, London or some other large urban hub that's convenient for the most people. Often it's at a luxury hotel where the studio has commandeered anywhere from a few rooms to an entire floor. The rooms are cleared of all furniture so they can build movie-specific sets for the stars, director or whoever is being interviewed. Each room has at least two chairs facing each other: one for the star, one for the journalist. There are two cameras and all the lighting and sound equipment needed for these positions. The number of people in the room, the proximity of chairs and the amount of equipment all conspire to make the rooms very claustrophobic. The lights heat up quickly and the comparison to a pressure cooker is pretty apt. There are many variations to this format, but that's the usual set-up.

Larger junkets are often broken up into a series of days – one day for the international press, one for domestic press and one for specialty events. The first two are self-explanatory, but the third requires some description as it has been growing in importance and frequency.

Specialty events used to be set aside for networks that sent their own crews as opposed to using the team provided by the studio. The network could create its own unique set and have more time with each celebrity. This was expensive for the network but paid off with unique footage that didn't look like everyone else's. Lately, however, many studios are moving away from specialty days and offering high-end, experiential events instead. In addition to a slot in the junket rotation, journalists are taken to an exotic location for a rare opportunity. They might, for example, learn etiquette and umbrella-warfare at the *Kingsman* press day in London, or take a jaunt down to the Ski Dome in Dubai for the *Scrat-Lympics* in support of *Ice Age*. The goal is to give journalists a spectacular experience that only this film can provide. The studio hopes that influencers will then write about the event, giving greater depth of engagement to their readers/viewers/followers.

The same thing used to be accomplished via *swag*.[3] That's what they call the premiums or giveaways that studios provide to journalists to help them remember the film. It could be as simple as a paperweight or t-shirt, or something elaborate like the *Cheaper By The Dozen Survival/First Aid Kit*. For many years there was a kind of arms race amongst studios to provide the coolest, cleverest, most expensive items at their junkets. I even received a leather jacket from the *Terminator 3* press day! Once it became expected, however, the practice started dying off. It still happens occasionally, but it's less common than it was.

---

[3] Pet peeve time. The word is pronounced as it's written – there is no "schw" in it. Don't say Schwag even though many people do, or you'll look green. The origin of swag is British, not Yiddish.

The junket is a great place to hone your skills as an interviewer. It's as fast and furious as basketball drills, and requires almost as much precision and stamina. You might conduct just one interview in a day, or six running from room to room. As frenetic as this sounds, it's extremely valuable as you can't help but get better at your job with this much repetition.

One inherent challenge at the junket, however, is the high chance for your partner to suffer from interview fatigue. I spoke with a young actor recently who starred in a summer blockbuster and had never done a junket before. He was told he'd be doing 150 interviews in one day! He was aghast, as you might expect. Remember, it's stressful on your partner as well.

ANYWHERE ELSE

If you're lucky enough to get exclusive time with your partner outside the junket environment, congratulations! Make the most of it. You now have the ability to design a creative environment and, budget allowing, a terrific looking set. It can be inside or outside, but I recommend the former. Shooting outside provides you with a great backdrop, but it's drastically more complicated, especially for audio. I've had to pause my interview for birds, airplanes, sirens, passersby, foghorns, jackhammers, flash-mobs… see what I mean? Of course, if you're interviewing a Nobel Prize-winning gardener (that's a thing, right?), being outside makes sense, but otherwise, do yourself a favor and stay indoors.

GET A ROOM – A BIG ONE

When choosing a location, you want a room that is at least twenty feet deep and ten feet wide. There's no upper limit as you can always carve out a corner if you have a vast sound stage to work with, but a small space can present problems.

It has to be big enough so that the camera can be ten feet or more from your partner. She should also be at least ten feet away from the back of your set so you can light the area between her and the background. This keeps her from looking flattened against the wall and helps a simple set look much better. The best way to confirm that you'll have enough space is to visit the location a couple days in advance. In other words:

BOOK A SCOUT

Remove a lot of stress from the day of your shoot by visiting your location in advance. I highly recommend this even if you aren't being paid for it (but try to get paid; you're not crazy). Plan your scout at least two days in advance so you have time to take advantage of what you learn, and bring your A-Team. Give yourself an hour or more at the location and come prepared with questions. You might need to add a generator for electricity, or better chairs for the interview. You might need additional PA's (production assistants) to lock up the background (keep people in a public space from walking into your shot), or any number of other variables. All will become known when you're at the location the first time.

Your Director of Photography (DP) and Line Producer should join you. You might also need your gaffer if it's a location not usually used for shooting. Bring your Art Director to assess the needs to dress the room or if you're building a set. In fact, bring any team member who will benefit and who you can afford – remember this is a workday for your crew.

While on location you'll want to get the feel of the space as well as nail down some logistics. The list of what you'll need to know will change on a case-by-case basis, but below is a list of questions that I start with. Make sure to add your own.

CHECKLIST – QUESTIONS TO ASK AT A SCOUT[4]

- √ Location address with zip code for GPS directions
- √ Name/phone number of your on-site contact
- √ What time can you arrive: 2 hours prior to shoot if possible/ 1 hour mandatory
- √ Where to load in/out equipment (loading dock/freight elevator, etc.)
- √ Parking info for you, your crew, your partner and her posse
- √ Where are the electrical outlets and can they handle the wattage? (Gaffer stuff)
- √ Will you need extra power or a generator? (Ditto)
- √ Where are the windows in the room, and can they be darkened?
- √ Overhead lights--fluorescent? (yuck) Can they be turned off or adjusted?
- √ Is there an air conditioner you can control for sound?
- √ Any ambient noise that might be a problem (street, neighbors, airplanes, etc.)?
- √ Is the room presentable or do you need to dress it/build a set?
- √ Are there hardwired phones nearby with ringers that can be turned off?

---

[4] Also available at GoodQuestionTheBook.com

- √ Is there a dumpster that you can use for your trash at load-out?
- √ Where is the closest bathroom or do you need to bring a porta-potty?
- √ Space to store your gear, feed your crew and make-up your partner?
- √ Some celebrities require their own green room or other private area they can use to relax between takes.
- √ Are there sprinkler systems and fire alarms? Production lights can set these off.
- √ Permits required? If it's a public space check with your local film office and they will guide you through the permitting process.
- √ Where is the closest hospital? For real.
- √ And most importantly, where is the nearest Starbucks so you can make sure everyone is properly caffeinated.

KEY TIP: TAKE PICTURES OF THE ROOM BEFORE YOU TOUCH ANYTHING.

There's never been a shoot in the history of history that didn't move something, so make sure you have a record of where everything belongs. Take lots of pictures before you touch a thing. Not only will this come in handy for sharing with team members who couldn't attend the scout, but it also serves to help you restore the room to its original state afterward. Make sure you've got Wide Shots from the four compass points, as well as specific Close-ups of furniture, lamps, etc. This is also a great way to stay on the good side of the person providing the location. You want a good report the day after your shoot so you're welcome back next time.

In the upcoming chapters I will go into much greater detail regarding both the junket and a shoot you produce "in your own house." Until then, to help you remember the high points, here is the checklist of what we've covered so far:

CHECKLIST: RESEARCH

√ Research Your Partner
- > Watch the movie/show she's promoting
- > Check official websites, fan sites, social media
- > Look at previous interviews she's done
- > Ask her handlers what will make her comfortable

√ Research The Venue
- > The Junket
  - Know what to expect about the process
  - Double check the street address and your time slot
  - Be familiar with your partner's work (It bears repeating)
- > Anywhere Else
  - Get a big room – 10' x 20' or bigger
  - Book a scout and ask a lot of questions
  - Take pictures of the room before moving anything

CHAPTER THREE

CRAFTING GOOD QUESTIONS

When my partner says, "Good question!" before answering, it's validation that all my preparation has paid off. It means that she is not only engaged, but considering her answers from a new perspective. Sometimes "good question!" precedes, "I don't know, let me think about that." Other times it means, "I was hoping someone would ask me that," or "yep, that's the crux of it, right there." Whatever it means, it's always a harbinger of authenticity and connection. *Getting there*, now that's the trick. Below I've outlined a number of strategies to help you earn this response.

WHERE TO START

Spend some time identifying the parameters of your interview and what you're after. What do you hope to get from your interview in terms of your finished piece? What would be your dream result, the perfect responses? As soon as you define your ultimate goal the shape of your interview will begin to appear. Start by asking yourself the following questions:

- **How long will I have with my partner? [Vital]**
- **How long will the finished piece be?**
- **What is the intended tone and audience of my piece?**
- **Do I need short, punchy answers or languid reminiscences?**

A NOTE ON TIMING

The first question above is the most important, so get used to asking it early. The answer to, "How long do I have with my partner?" is going to affect almost everything: from the kind of energy you'll bring into the room, to the number of questions you'll get to ask, to the order and way in which you ask them. Obviously a three-minute interview is a different animal than a thirty-minute encounter, so be prepared for whatever happens.

In all cases, front-load your list of questions with the ones you really need. You never know when someone is running late and your interview gets cut short. A circuit breaker could trip and you're done for the day. A publicist could decide your partner is tired and you only get one more question. These things have happened to me, and many more unforeseeable events. You don't want to scramble to reorder your questions while you're sitting across from your partner, so make sure you lead off with your heavy hitters.

On the flip side, have enough questions to cover your time <u>and then some</u>. Steve Martin once answered all of my questions in two minutes, and I had twice that much time left with him. I had back-ups so I didn't waste the opportunity, thank goodness. A rough estimate is: each question and answer will take between one and three minutes. If you get four questions asked and answered in five minutes, you're lucky, but that's just an estimate. Make sure you go into a five-minute interview with *ten* questions, just in case you sit down with Mr. Martin.

MAKE YOUR QUESTIONS YOUR OWN

Some clients write your questions for you and want you to ask them verbatim. Other times you'll write your own questions, either with or without your client's guidance. Most often it's somewhere in between. Your client might give you the points she wants you to cover, but getting there is your business. This is actually the best-case scenario because you want your questions to sound like you.

You're going to sound the most natural if you use your own words. Usually that only takes a little massaging, but there are occasions when it's major surgery. I once worked with a client who handed me a question that read, "Please expand on the ROI of leveraging the digital space this fiscal versus last." I worked with him to humanize this and together we revised it to, "What new things are you doing on social media?" Give your client what she wants but remember you're being hired for your expertise. Since Rule #1 is to make the interview sound like a conversation, guide your client to let you do just that.

Then make sure you understand what each question is really after. If you don't write the questions yourselves, it's easy to miss this step. Ask your client to explain any complex issues in advance so that you're well-informed on the subject. Otherwise you could be caught flat-footed when your partner looks at you with a blank stare and says, "…Uh, what do you mean by that?" It's on you to rephrase it more simply. To that end, run through the questions with your client in advance and ask for any clarification. This is also a good time to find out which questions are priorities if there are any time issues (as in always).

DON'T BE TONE DEAF

The same question can be asked many different ways in different circumstances. There's a massive difference between the interview you do for an in-depth documentary, and one for a comic man-on-the-street piece. Let your tone be your guide. Are you producing a think piece, or a light-hearted marketing spot? Are you appealing to young children, financial executives or the general public? Do you end with a call-to-action or a punch line? The earlier you decide on the tone, the better you'll be able to gauge the style, length and substance of your questions. Sometimes it's that obvious, but other times it's a judgment call.

I was interviewing a well-known actor for a horror/comedy web series and I started asking some pretty basic questions when he stopped and demanded, "Why are you doing it like that?" I realized he was right and tried to pivot to a more appropriate tone on the spot. My audience would be expecting something funny or weird, and I was doing basic. Keep your audience in the back of your mind to make sure you're speaking to them. The tone of the film, show or talent will be your first indicator. Jack Black, for example, isn't going to want to discuss his deep, Method-based acting process. He's going want to screw around, and you're a fool if you don't let him. It's sort of like dressing for a funeral vs. a cocktail party. Just knowing the occasion is enough to prepare you for the right tone; getting it wrong could be disastrous.

START WITH SOFTBALLS, THEN TURN UP THE HEAT

Unless you're going to be at a junket with the commensurate extreme time pressure, get a dialogue going before asking anything too profound. I start with something easy like, "This looked like a lot of fun to work on." That's not even a question, but my first goal is to establish a rapport. Next I like to go for a timeline, even a loose one like, "When did you first hear about this project?" or "How long have you been working on this?" Getting my partner thinking back to the beginning of the process gives my finished piece a coherent structure. She may give me simple facts or head off on a tangent of some kind. I'm happy with either. A few minutes into the interview is when I ask the big-ticket items like:

- **What is it about this part that really moved you?**
- **What did you do to prepare for the role?**
- **What did you do each day to get into character?**

Once you've got your partner talking, go into the details of the specific project. Let the discussion flow wherever it wants to, and sneak a look at your list to see if you're hit any of your questions without asking them. Keep it natural and ride your partner's enthusiasm to whatever comes up.

The one type of question I don't recommend is the, "would you *say something more* about that" or "talk to me about…" format. It's a style of last resort, if you ask me that indicates you have either not done your preparation or are out of ideas. More than anything, it's completely unnatural to an authentic conversation. Can you imagine someone saying to you over drinks: *"Talk a little about your kidney stones."* Doesn't happen.

Then, wrap it up with another softball that will give you a good ending, like:

- **How do you feel it all turned out?**
- **What do you hope the audience will walk away with?**
- **What will you remember most about this experience?**

This *start slow* approach is fine if you have the time. In a junket scenario, however, you may have to go for the jugular right away. If so, try and soften your approach with something disarming like, "I have so little time, let's jump right in – why this role?" I hate to do that, but celebrities are used to it, so it usually works out fine. The key is to keep the tone fun and chatty. Use your natural abilities and the tips that follow to get there.

KEY TIP: KEEP YOUR QUESTIONS SHORT SO HER ANSWERS CAN BE LONG.

To quote the musical *Hamilton*, "Talk less. Smile more." Unless you're going to be on-camera, long questions are time-consuming at best and confusing at worst. Plus most people only answer the last part of a complex question so don't give them a novel as a run-up. This takes some practice. After you've crafted your questions shorten them to the fewest number of words possible. Aim for questions that fit onto a single line. Emulate Hemingway, not Dickens.

For example, I had originally written this:

You're known for submerging yourself in complex characters and making each one so different that you seem like a different actor each time, complete with voice training and physicality. What did you do, this time, to achieve that goal?

In the heat of the moment, I realized I didn't need all that preamble. Instead I asked, "How did you prepare for this role?" It worked great. I got everything I needed and kept the focus where it belongs: on my partner.

KEY TIP: NO "YES/NO."

Monosyllabic answers are a nightmare. A 'yes' or 'no' gives you nothing to work with in post. To prevent this, make sure your questions are open-ended. Adapt your question from "Did you enjoy working on this film?" or "did you know about this book before it became a movie?" to "*Why* did you want to work on this film?" and "*How much* did you know about this subject?" Small difference; big results. You don't want this:

> **Reese Witherspoon (half-serious): I only answer yes/no questions.**
>
> **KR: (playing along) Oh, really, why is that?**
>
> **Reese (laughing) Yes!**

Beyond hamstringing you in the post process, yes/no answers sometimes signal that your partner is not interested in talking to you. Don't take it personally. She might just be having a bad day. She might be bored. She might even not speak English perfectly.

It could be almost anything, and it's rarely your fault. The best/worst example of this is probably the infamous "7 Awkward Minutes" with the late, great, sometimes irate Jerry Lewis you can find online. I go into some detail about this in Chapter Twelve, but feel free to Google it in advance for a preview of the worst-case scenario. It's both instructive and chilling at the same time.

EYES UP

A good interview is an unpredictable human interaction that flows organically between different subjects. Your interview should feel like two people talking, not like one person reading a list to the other. Just like any good speaker at a podium, get your eyes off your paper as much as possible. Make eye contact with your partner and stay there.

I think of my questions as notes or talking points, not as a script. They're reminders of what I want to cover but have very little to do with the actual order in which I ask them. Don't just move on to a new subject as soon as your question is answered satisfactorily. That's not a conversation, that's a deposition. Instead, hit your marks, guide the discussion and be ready to improvise. Sneak a peak at your notes, but keep your eyes off the page and go with the flow.

Listen carefully and notice which subjects she warms to. Even more important than factual answers, you want engagement and energy. The best way to inspire that is to let your partner talk about something she's truly interested in. You don't want her to ramble, but that's not usually a problem (ok, sometimes). Once you've brought up your important topics, let the dialogue flow naturally.

KEY TIP: PRINT YOUR QUESTIONS AND PUT THEM ON A CLIPBOARD.

If you've ever tried to write on a single piece of paper on your lap, you probably have the puncture wounds to prove it. A clipboard or a notebook will protect against this as well as keep your paper from making noise. It may be old school, but it works. Bringing a tablet or computer into the room is cumbersome and can interfere with lighting and, especially, sound. I have a very nice, butcher-block clipboard that I've used for years. Don't be shy about devoting a couple of bucks toward making yourself look more professional, while solving a very practical issue at the same time.

CHECKLIST: CRAFTING GOOD QUESTIONS

√ Know the parameters of your interview
- > How long will you have?
- > What is the tone
- > Who is the audience?
- > Will you be on-camera or not?
- > Do you need long or short answers?

√ Write your questions carefully
- > Put your most important questions at the top
- > Have enough questions to cover the time
- > Write them in your own voice

- > Keep them short
- > Don't ask Yes/No questions
- > Keep your eyes off your paper
- > Start easy, then turn up the heat (unless you're at a junket)
- > Be ready to jump around your list
- > Use a clipboard or notebook

CHAPTER FOUR

SHORTCUTS AND TRICKS

Like any good coach, I stress the value of preparation and repetition until you know your game inside and out. This includes knowing your partner, staying alert, and allowing your interview to go wherever it wants (within reason). Those are the basics. Now here are some shortcuts I've discovered that work surprising well. Shhh, don't tell anyone I told you...

SHORTCUT #1 - DECIDE IN ADVANCE WHAT YOU WANT YOUR PARTNER TO SAY.

Come up with a list of *it-would-be-perfect-if-she-said* lines, and then <u>back</u> into them. For example, if you want, "I did this film because it explores a combative divorce, and that's something I'm pretty familiar with," then ask, "What resonated with you about this role?" Sometimes it's that simple. If you don't get the answer you're looking for, keep probing: "Is there an issue this film brings up that speaks to you personally?" No one will blame you for leading the witness. What's uncool in a courtroom is perfectly kosher in an interview setting.

SHORTCUT #2 - WRITE THE PREFERRED ANSWERS NEXT TO YOUR QUESTIONS.

This will keep your specific goals top of mind. I put them in brackets after each question like, "How long did you train for this part?" [*It took two years to learn the karate moves.*] This is incredibly helpful during the interview as you can tick off what you've gotten as well as what you still need. There is an exception to this shortcut, however. Sometimes you will be asked to share your questions with your partner in advance. In that case, simply keep two versions of your questions, one with and one without the answers.

SHORTCUT #3 - FOOTNOTE THE ANSWERS.

This is really the same as above, writing out the answers on your questions doc, but it looks more literary. I've had clients ask for this format specifically because it's easier to get approved, for some reason. Just insert a footnote number after your question and write the answer you want in the footer.[5] One advantage to this is it gives you a concise list of everything you're after, making it easy to scan during the interview.

---

[5] Yeah, like this.

SHORTCUT #4 - WRITE OUT A COMPLETE SCRIPT OF THE FINISHED INTERVIEW AND HAVE YOUR PARTNER ACTUALLY READ IT.

I know this sounds about as spontaneous as an airplane safety announcement but it's the exception that proves the rule. I suggested this to a client once before interviewing his boss's boss. We needed to make sure there were no surprises and this seemed to be a failsafe. After conducting my usual interview, I asked his boss to read my script right off the page. Surprisingly he was only too happy to comply and, it worked great. Now this client insists on this process every time.

I try and split the difference, however. I conduct a traditional interview first and hope to get some or all of the answers in my partner's own spontaneous words. Then, once we're done, I hand over the script and ask her to read the parts I'm missing. This comes in handy when you have extremely specific or technical language or when your partner suffers from:

KEY TIP: *RED LIGHT FEVER*

"Red light fever" is what you call a change in personality when you point a camera at someone. Some people freeze up. Others get chatty and start *performing*, losing all their spontaneity. Others get terribly shy or tongue-tied or flushed or any one of a dozen other reactions that get in the way of an authentic interview. It's rare in actors, but comes up occasionally with directors, executives, writers, anyone not used to being in front of the camera.

To address this, turn the camera off and make an honest connection. Share something about yourself to start, and get your partner talking about a topic she really loves--dogs, family, ice cream—anything. Once you've established a rapport you can start over and roll the camera. If the fever spikes again, put a piece of tape over the red light and tell your partner you're not rolling. It's a little sneaky, but it often does the trick.

TRICKS

What's the difference between a trick and a shortcut? I hear you ask. *Shortcuts* are strategic, big-picture approaches to an entire interview. *Tricks* are tactical and aimed at overcoming specific obstacles. Below are a few approaches to unique problems that you may have to deal with.

TRICK #1 - THE POWER OF WHY?

This is the one question that I have used in almost every interview I've ever done; yet it has never appeared on any of my lists. It's the key to getting past rote answers and prepared statements, as well as the best way to make an interview feel like a conversation. When you're not getting what you need or you think your partner has more to say on a subject, follow up with this simple rejoinder. Did she just pause in the middle of her answer as if she remembered something important? This question digs out what it was. Did she laugh before she answered, and then give you a serious, polished response? This question uncovers what's so funny. This simple, monosyllabic query has led to more *Good Questions!*'s than any other technique, so it's worth remembering. More about this in Chapter Seven but it's so valuable I wanted to bring it up early. It's an incredibly powerful tool and one interviewers often forget to use effectively. It was also the runner-up for title of this book.

TRICK #2 – THE PREGNANT PAUSE.

Journalists have been using this trick for ages. When you're confronted with what sounds like a pat answer and you want to go deeper, one way to get there is the pregnant pause. Retain eye contact, hold your breath for a second *and wait*. This signals to your partner that you know there's something more. If you stay connected and don't say a word, it's amazing how often she'll volunteer more information, usually in greater depth. A pregnant pause is different than a simple break in the discussion in that it is *filled* with anticipation. You're signaling, non-verbally, that you're waiting for the other shoe to drop. It's a pause full of meaning and expectation and once you get good at it, you won't need to think through the mechanics. Until then, here are some steps you can take:

- **Look up from your notes and lock eyes**
- **Lean forward slightly**
- **Raise your eyebrows or cock your head slightly as if to say, "…and?"**
- **Let a faint smile creep over your lips as if you're awaiting for a punch line**
- **Even hold your breath slightly**

It's a surprisingly effective trick, which is why it's been around for so long. One word of caution – don't wait too long. If nothing is forthcoming, move on.

TRICK #3 – ASK THE OPPOSITE.

One of my favorite ways of getting my partner to say something I need is to pose the opposite scenario as if I think she'll agree. The goal is to get an emphatic rebuttal in order to correct me. Here's what I mean:

> KR: What was the hardest part of preparing to play Amelia Earhart?
>
> HILARY SWANK: The physicality and the accent.
>
> KR: Oh, so you just concentrated on those things and let the cameras roll?
>
> HILARY SWANK: NO. No, once you've done all your research and you've done all that preparation, it's then *in* you, and you just have to trust that it's there and then let go, so that you can *play* with the other actors and really collaborate.

TRICK #4 - THE TRUTH ABOUT CONSEQUENCES.

One of my clients is insistent that I always include the question, "What would have been the *consequences* if you hadn't [... *spent time near an actual volcano* / ... *rehearsed with the real lizards* / ... *learned to swallow a sword*...]. It raises the stakes from a casual reference to an integral part of her process. Sometimes it takes a few tries to get your partner to see where you're going. Make sure you have the perfect answer in your head so you know how to guide her if needed.

TRICK #5 - FIRST, THEN, FINALLY.

Another handy tool is to get a timeline from your partner. Remember that you're creating a story that needs a beginning, middle and end. Make sure you have the building blocks you need to support that.

> **MONICA SWANN:** *First* we had to find the right actors and that took... And *then* we needed our screenwriter to adjust a few things for our unique talent, and... *Finally* all the pieces were in place and the director signed off...

You want this to sound natural so don't be too strict about the wording. Make mental (or literal) notes during your interview to make sure you have what you need. I've even gone so far as to ask my partner to actually say the words, "First... Next... Then... And finally..." with a pause between each. Don't be shy to get these little pieces, the same way on set you might shoot inserts or cut-aways. They may seem random and disjointed at the time but, trust me, you'll be glad you have them and your editor will be thrilled.

BE READY FOR ANYTHING

It may seem counter-intuitive, but the more prepared you are, the easier it is to be spontaneous. Actors are taught this basic technique: do your homework, prepare the best you can, and when it's time to perform: let it go and have fun, whatever comes your way.

A perfect example of this happened to a colleague of mine. He was interviewing Charlize Theron for her role in *Mad Max: Fury Road*. When they met, he was struck by her intelligence, charisma and true star quality while, at the same time, by what a no-nonsense professional she was. My friend had done his homework, so he was able to master his intimidation and get to work. He settled in, struck a professional tone and asked his first question, "What characteristics define 'Furiosa' as a heroine?"

She responded with exactly the opposite answer than he was anticipating. She felt that her character was not a heroine in the strict sense. And that took the wind out of his sails. Unfortunately, the rest of his questions were based on this first one. Now what could he do? He could listen. He was smart and nimble enough to let the conversation flow naturally and it paid off. They discussed topics totally different to the ones that he had planned, and got a perfectly unique interview.

My friend is a network executive with a lot of people who reviewed his work afterward. They were delighted. Charlize had given him surprising answers, different than any other journalist got, and with an authentic and unique angle. What could be better? He knew something it takes many of us years to learn: preparation is great, but authenticity is everything. Bottom line: know your material well enough to be flexible, and embrace the surprises.

CHECKLIST: SHORTCUTS & TRICKS

√ Shortcuts

- > What exactly do you want your partner to say?
- > Write your dream answers next to your questions or as footnotes
- > Or: have your partner read a complete script

√ Tricks

- > The Power of Why
- > The pregnant pause
- > Ask the opposite
- > Consequences?
- > Timeline – "first, then, finally…"

√ Embrace Surprises

Section Two

 # PRODUCTION

THE ROOM WHERE IT HAPPENS

PART ONE

AT THE JUNKET

CHAPTER FIVE

ARRIVAL

Now let's take a look at the nuts and bolts of the junket experience. A press junket is a unique environment where the studio handles almost everything for you. They book the crew, build the sets, create the schedules, arrange the parking and even supply lunch! All you have to do is show up on time and comport yourself like a pro.

Your first stop is a room they usually call the Hospitality Suite. Check in at the desk and politely verify that they have name and outlet correct. Confirm the time you are scheduled to meet the talent. Double-check whether you have a single slot (five minutes), or a double (ten). Feel free to ask if they're on schedule as these events can get backed up, and they'll have the most recent updates. Just don't be a noodge.

Once you know how long you have before your interview, find a quiet place to chill until you're called. It could be five minutes or two hours. Waiting can be nerve wracking, so bring something to do. Don't get caught up in the kvetching that sometimes goes on among jaded journalists who have always seen this done better. Be sociable, but if the chatter takes a turn toward the unproductive, excuse yourself and go over your questions. That kind of energy can seep into your mood, and subtly hamstring you. Have fun, stay positive and focus on your task, even if it means a little self-quarantine.

It is not uncommon to be asked to trade your time with someone who has to catch a plane or has some other conflict. If so, I recommend helping out a fellow journalist whenever possible. It pays to be cool, and you might just need a favor yourself someday. That is, unless there's a chance you'll lose your spot entirely. If so, politely decline. Sometimes your partner is late and that means someone has to get bumped. If you have a slot late in the day, you could find yourself out of luck; I have. It's crummy, but it happens. Therefore always request the earliest time slot possible. This is also beneficial if your partner gets bored with her long day. The sweet spots are when she first arrives and soon after lunch.

CARDINAL RULES

Don't let the first class treatment fool you. Even in these high-end surroundings, there is pressure on all sides at a junket. If you can lower it, even a little, you'll be rewarded with extra consideration, future invitations and maybe even longer slots. If you make things worse, there's a fair chance you won't be invited back. When they have to cut someone from the rotation, repeat offenders are the first to go. Be one of the good guys and make sure you follow a few simple, self-explanatory rules:

- **Be on time**
- **Don't go over your time limit in the room**
- **Avoid asking the celebrities questions that are off-limits**

KEY TIP: BE RESPECTFUL OF THE JUNKET STAFF.

This may seem like a no-brainer, but many people treat these hard-working professionals like volunteers at a bake sale. Not only is that rude, it's dumb. You want to keep these folks happy, so make sure you show your appreciation for their help. There is often a hair/make-up station set up as well. If you're going to be on-camera yourself, make sure to avail yourself of their services. Even if you're not on-camera, it never hurts to check in and let them give you a quick sprucing up to make sure you're presentable. Don't take them for granted either as these are skilled professionals too.

KEY TIP: IF YOU'RE EARLY, TAKE A FIELD TRIP TO THE MACHINE ROOM.

A great way to get an edge before your interview is to poke your head into the machine room where technicians are monitoring the interviews. Don't ask *if* you can look in because the staff might answer, "Um--I don't know--just to be safe: No." This is one of those *easier to get forgiveness than permission* situations. Just ask where it is, "for when I'm done" and quietly slip down there like you have an appointment.

The machine room is a large space full of monitors, technicians and gear which looks a little like a mini-Mission Control. The people there make sure that all the cameras are running properly, the audio is pristine and the picture is consistent. It is also where they record and duplicate your media to give to you when you're done. They may provide a flashcard, a thumb drive or whatever the latest technology is. Lately they're posting the media to a secure server for easy downloading.

Be a fly on the wall and look for the feed coming from the room you'll be entering (there may be many others). See what the shot looks like: how wide is it, what's in the background, is the name of the film in the shot? Most importantly how does your partner look? I've had occasions where the star had changed her appearance so much I didn't recognize her. Rachel McAdams had platinum blond hair at a junket I attended, but in the film she was a brunette. Her new hair color changed her look so much it took me a minute to register it was her.

Catching a sneak peek from the machine room takes away one beat of surprise. Get a feeling for your partner's energy. Look for any clues before you enter the room so you have an edge. This is a unique preview; don't underestimate its value.

KEY TIP: BE READY FOR DEPLOYMENT.

After your reconnaissance mission, get back to the Hospitality Suite as soon as possible and let them know you've returned. The last thing you want is to make the staff wait for you so keep your field trip short. Schedules get shuffled around and you don't want to be skipped.

By the way, there's always a ton of food in the hospitality suite, often themed to the film they're promoting, and it's usually the hotel's better fare. My advice, however, is to eat after you're done with your interview. No one wants to talk to you with parsley in your teeth.

Once your time is called, you'll be sent to a specific room where your partner is stationed. Outside that room is another studio employee as well as three to six journalists waiting in a row of chairs for their turns. This is called being *on deck*, and feels like sitting in the belly of a paratroop plane lined up for a jump. Go over your questions again.

THE BLESSING OF NERVOUS ENERGY

Don't be surprised if you are nervous before your interview. Anytime you step into a room filled with people, equipment, a famous partner and a ticking clock it's bound to be a little nerve-wracking. Your heart rate goes up, you become hyper-vigilant and you might experience something similar to stage fright. Do what performers do under these circumstances and *use it*.

You are experiencing something primal akin to the fight-or-flight response. It's nature's way of sharpening your wits. Be grateful for the rush of adrenaline and let it focus your thoughts and broaden your perceptions. This is a temporary state--a super power really that, while it may feel a little odd, is an amazing gift.

The challenge is that this kind of energy can make you a little frenetic. Learning to control it is one of the stepping-stones to conducting great interviews. These feelings happen to everyone at some point, so it helps to be prepared. There are many tricks to mitigate stage fright or the feeling of being star struck (which can affect you the same way). Some people just ignore it (I don't recommend that), others imagine their partner in their underwear. But I find the best solution is activity.

Don't sit down. Stand up, pace, shake out your hands. If you have the room, do some stretches, jumping jacks or run in place. Don't get all sweaty, but channel that pent up adrenaline into your muscles where it belongs. Imagine energy running out from your fingertips and toes. This won't stop the butterflies, it will do something better: focus and tame them. You want all this energy working for you and this gets it moving in a useful direction. The one thing I don't recommend is engaging with the other journalists. That can distract you from your goal. Keep your head in the game and you can chat afterwards. Go over your questions, get active and don't worry about the butterflies; they're here to help.

KEY TIP: IF YOU'RE NOT NERVOUS, GET THERE.

When you first start out, unless you're some steely-eyed ninja, you're bound to be a little nervous at a junket. In fact, if you're not, you're probably not ready. If you're not in a proper state of heightened (but not manic) attention – get yourself there. Step outside for some air. Shake your hands out as if they were wet. Get physical in some way. Raise your heart rate. These are exactly the same exercises that will help if you're *too* nervous, so I recommend them before each interview no matter how you feel. I like the image of a pot of water simmering, not quite boiling, but with the lid on tightly. All that energy is there, but no one can see it because it's controlled. Don't let it throw it you; it's just your engine idling at the starting gate.

STATE-DEPEDENT MEMORY

Rehearsing *while* you're nervous will give you an incredible advantage. Behavioral scientists call this State-Dependent Memory. The theory posits that we execute things best when we learn them under similar circumstances to their real-life application. For example, if you study for a test slightly caffeinated, you'll do better on the test if you have a cup of coffee first. If you're going to be conducting an interview in a high-pressure environment like a junket, there's no better time to practice your questions than right before you walk in the door. You're already in a state of heightened awareness.

I availed myself of this practice when I was directing a young actress with a challenge ahead of her. She was going to have to read her lines straight to camera right after a bucket of cold, green goo was dumped on her head![6] The shot was going to be a giant mess, and we only had one chance to capture it. If she went up (forgot her lines) we were in trouble. I decided to help her out with a little state-dependent memory.

While the crew set up the shot, I asked the actress to step to the side and rehearse her lines again. Unseen, I placed a small stepladder behind her, climbed up and dropped a few hand towels on her head while she was working. At first she was startled and couldn't remember a single line, as I'd suspected. We did it a few more times and, after the initial surprise wore off, she was ready. When it came time for the slime, she gave a spirited and fun performance, and was letter perfect on her dialogue.

Get that initial shock out of the way by rehearsing under real-life stress. Then give yourself a task, like concentrating on your first few questions. Make priorities like "make sure I get her to say her character's name" or "keep it fun, not somber" or anything else that is appropriate to your goals. Then go over your questions *again* in this rarefied condition.

---

[6] This ritual is called getting slimed in Nickelodeon parlance. For more details, ask a ten-year-old.

CHAPTER SIX

GETTING STARTED

WHEN 5 = 3 AND 10 = 8

The main challenge you'll face at a junket is the extreme time pressure. If you have a spot in the rotation, you'll usually get five minutes with your partner. This is called a "single." Realistically it's probably closer to three or four minutes. On special occasions, the studio may grant you a "double," which is ostensibly ten minutes, but is really more like seven or eight. The studio's goal is to introduce the artists to as many media outlets as possible in a limited amount of time. Since interviewers often go over their allotment, and there is no margin for error, the studio severely limits each time slot.

Inside the room, along with your partner and the crew, there's one more person who will always be present: The Time Keeper. She stands behind your partner, right in your eye-line, and rules the room with an iron stopwatch. During your interview she holds up fingers indicating how many minutes you have left. As you approach your limit she starts circling her hand to signal: WRAP IT UP, PAL. That circle gets faster and faster, gradually turning into a fist. I might have imagined that but she's pretty insistent. You both have a job to do and with some practice, you can work together effectively, get what you need and still get out on time.

RAMP UP QUICKLY

Bring a *contained energy* with you into the room and quickly scope out the environment. Is it hot from all the lights? Is your partner slumped in her chair, exhausted, or chatting energetically with the crew? You're on the clock, so do this quickly.

Greet your partner and introduce yourself before you sit down. It never hurts to compliment her work, but don't fawn. Celebrities can recognize fake adulation a mile away, so keep it professional. I usually shake hands, but not everyone wants to do that. I've met more than one celebrity who is germ-conscious and doesn't like to be touched by strangers all day long. Read the signals and act appropriately.

For most interviews, the finished product will not include you or your questions on-camera. That means you have to make sure your partner answers in, as we called it in elementary school, a complete sentence. To avoid a lengthy discussion on grammar simply ask her to, "Please incorporate my questions into your answers." This adjustment seems like it will add a layer of artificiality to your discussion, but most celebrities are used to it.

Get your partner talking as soon as possible. Once she starts, you can breathe and gather your thoughts as you decide where to go next. Your second question may or may not be the second on your list, depending on how quickly you get into a real conversation.

GROUND RULES

If you have any special requirements for your interview, let your partner know right away. Such housekeeping issues might include asking her to:

- ID herself at the top: "I'm ___ and I play ___ in ___?" [See caution below]

- **Speak to you, not directly into camera [unless…**

- **You have any tags, liners or shout-outs you need which *do* go straight to camera**

Above all, reinforce that, "This is just a conversation" so she doesn't feel she has to speak in banner headlines or without pauses. Do all this before your time starts if possible.

KEY TIP: BE CAREFUL ASKING FOR ID'S.

The bigger the star, the more likely they're not going to ID themselves on-camera. I had a manager break into the middle of my interview advising my partner not to do so. I had an actor I won't mention stare at me as if I hadn't asked him anything at all and eat up almost a minute of my precious time. I even had a conscientious client tell me to dispense with this question when interviewing a very famous, but thorny director. He wanted me to "come back alive." Ask for it if you need it, but don't be surprised if you're turned down.

LEAD WITH CONFIDENCE, NOT EGO

Have the confidence to direct your partner, and then get out of the way. Ask your questions clearly and succinctly, then sit back and let her digest them. Don't feel you have to jump in and save her if she doesn't answer immediately. Quick answers are usually prepared answers, so allow her to pause and think if need be.

Often performers are tired and need some pepping up. If so, lead with your energy and don't get sucked into theirs. On the other hand there are performers whose manic energy can hardly be contained like Jim Carrey or the late, great Robin Williams. Interviewing these comic masterminds felt like stepping onto a moving roller coaster. All I could do was hang on and have a blast! They knew exactly what they're doing, and that pace worked for them so I didn't try to compete.

MAKE A CONNECTION

Don't be afraid to look your partner in the eye and wait for her to do the same. Actors usually respond positively to eye contact. It's powerful, infectious and gives you a firm connection. Many interviewers miss this opportunity and bury their gaze in their list, losing a direct link to their partner. This is the reason I suggest you memorize, or at least super-familiarize yourself with your first three questions. Every time you look at your list, you're breaking the connection, so don't do it at the top of your interview.

When you sit face to face with someone and really listen, you can't help but feel a bond. If you're lucky, this will manifest itself in your partner revealing honest, authentic information. This bond can be achieved in a number of ways and you'll know it by the subtle signals. Your partner's answers get deeper and more candid. The tone of her voice may change and you suddenly feel like you're chatting with an old friend. That's exactly where you want to be.

I asked Mark Wahlberg what had led him to acting and stayed on the subject beyond his first answer. He surprised me by discussing being incarcerated when he was young. I doubt it was one of the talking points he'd intended to share that day. That kind of candor and honesty is a gift for which I was extremely grateful.

I found myself feeling downright paternal toward Leonardo DiCaprio, because his jacket was wrinkled at the shoulders. I gave him the tip from *Broadcast News* about sitting on the tail of his coat. He did it, and sincerely thanked me in a tone I hadn't heard in my interview. He appreciated my looking out for him, and from then on we were *in this together*. Yeah, I made Leonardo DiCaprio look good. You're welcome America.

Maybe the most memorable connection I ever had was with Kirk Douglas after his stroke. His speech was impaired and he was hard to understand at first. Ever the fighter, he soldiered on. He had a gleam in his eye and tackled each question with passion. I took my time and curtailed my questions to whatever he was comfortable with. He struggled with every word, and won every struggle. How could you not love a guy like that? Of course, *he* is Spartacus.

GET THE BIG PICTURE

There's an enormous difference between hearing someone, and really listening to her. The latter bears incredible fruit, and the first step is awareness. Take a moment to look at the whole person. Observe her posture first, and then try and hone in on some details. Scan for tension in the muscles of her jaw. Are her eyes wandering around the room? Is she leaning forward, fully engaged or sitting back nervously flicking her nails? Is she, God forbid, crossing her arms? If signs of tension are apparent, you have an obstacle to overcome. Luckily you can do something about this.

If you want your partner to be more comfortable, start by adjusting your own body language. No actor can resist working with someone who's truly excited to be there – it's contagious. Sit up straight, plant your feet on the floor, lean in and focus. She'll pick up these cues from you and, if you're fully engaged, she'll respond in kind.

Being aware of more than just your partner's words is vital if, on occasion, you stray into an uncomfortable area. I was once interviewing a major movie star who had been famous all of his life. I was tasked with exploring his acting process. In the course of our interaction I noticed something odd. My first question on the subject was met with a facile, tossed-off response. As I pursued the details, he started "stimming," – his legs were crossed and the foot in the air started tapping. He must have noticed it because he changed the cross of his legs. No good. Before long the other foot started doing it. I didn't want to abandon my goal (I'd come all the way to Cannes), so I came at it from another direction. He put both feet on the ground to stop the mid-air tap dance and concentrated. In a few minutes, however, he slipped one foot out of his shoe, and then put it back on, over and over again. Soon he was doing it with the other shoe too. His answers were getting more and more general and disjointed. His eyes were wandering around the room as if he were looking to escape. I knew I was not going to get much more on this subject and, worse than that, I was clearly torturing the poor guy.

This surprised me given that he was an Oscar-winning actor, but some people are not great at discussing their process. I'm not an investigative journalist grilling the White House Press Secretary, so there was no point in making him squirm, literally. I moved on to easier topics and he calmed down. His footwear stayed in place for the rest of the interview.

Remember: you're on the same side. There are plenty of gotcha journalists out there, and celebrities fear and despise them. Make sure your partners knows you're not one of them. Even the kindest of celebrities will often have their guard up. Tom Hanks once answered my innocent question in this beguilingly defensive way:

> KR: Are there any subjects you don't discuss with certain types of people?
>
> TOM HANKS (smiling): Sure, anything personal with journalists.

TREAT YOUR PARTNER LIKE A FRIEND

Make your partner feel like she is important to you personally. You don't have to fake anything, you just have to be present and the rest will take care of itself. Use this as an opportunity to really support her and you can't go wrong. If she is a serious person, match her tone. If she's gregarious, enjoy her energy and play along. And if she wants to play – join her.

I was at the junket for the animated *Treasure Planet* and I walked into a room with Martin Short while he was in the middle of a game. He and the crew were trying to name songs that had numbers in the title, each corresponding to how many more interviews he had left to do. I was third-to-last for the day, so our number was three. I dove right in and suggested *Mack The Knife*. It doesn't haven a number in the title, but it does come from *Three Penny Opera* so I hoped it counted. It did. I didn't win a prize, but I won over my partner and we had a great time from then on. The timekeeper didn't even start the clock until the game was over because Martin had initiated it. Phew. If you join the game, you're on the team.

CHAPTER SEVEN

LISTEN ACTIVELY

L earn to listen in every way that you can: with your ears, your eyes and your mind. Notice what your partner is saying, as well as how she's saying it, and what she *isn't* saying. Was there a pause that sounded like something just occurred to her? Did she consciously omit something you could pursue? What is her body language telling you? Is she looking you in the eye or avoiding your gaze? If you make eye contact and pay attention, you'll know when to pursue something and when to move on.

KEY TIP: RESPOND WITH YOUR EYES, YOUR FACE AND YOUR BODY.

Great answers can be elicited non-verbally, and this ability is one of the most important to cultivate from this entire book. To hone this skill, try an exercise: have someone tell you a complicated story that you don't already know (directions to a distant location works well). As you listen, try to understand every detail of the story *without* asking any questions. The trick isn't to sew your mouth shut and concentrate as hard as you can, it's to communicate your questions non-verbally. Let your expression and body language signal when you understand, when you agree and when you're not sure what she means.

This ability is helpful in an interview where you can't always interject, "Oh?...uh-huh...right..." as you would during a friendly chat. That absence can make things feel stagey. Fill in the gaps with smiles, nods and facial expressions that let your partner know you're not just listening, you're involved. The tiniest tilt of the head or furrowed brow communicates very clearly, "What do you mean?" A smile can suggest, "I get it, go on...". Leaning forward in your chair will infer that you want to hear more about this fascinating story. You can even laugh silently. Feel free to react to her jokes and off-hand remarks with what looks like comedy mime.

Paying attention to your partner's physical cues has the added benefit of getting you out of your own head. If you're concentrating on what she's saying, you won't be self-conscious about the sound of your own voice, whether you chose the right shirt or if your next question is lame. You'll be in the moment. This focus keeps you present and authentic while subtly encouraging your partner to do the same.

Once you get good at this, you can even get your partner to answer a question without actually asking it. If your partner is rambling, you can pull her back with an expression that communicates, "I lost you there." She wants to be clear so she'll go back and re-phrase. If she doesn't, you can always ask a follow-up but it's much better if it comes from her. I reward a successful explanation with a big smile which reads "Aha, that's so *interesting*" without mucking up the audio. Don't worry, you're not faking it, you're controlling it.

FEEL IT, DON'T' FAKE IT

And on the subject of faking—contrary to popular belief, actors are trained to *access* their emotions, not to fake them. If your partner is relating something emotional, you may very well feel it too. Don't be afraid to let her know. Don't put on an act, but don't put up a barrier either. You don't have to *do* anything, just be there with her. Maintain eye contact; nod if it feels appropriate; be yourself. You are an emotional spotter, ready to support her if she needs it. If she were a good friend, you wouldn't shy away from the hard stuff. You would let her know you're there for her and giver her your full attention. The same rules apply here.

When this level of intimacy is achieved, stay there as long as it seems appropriate. Be grateful for the trust your partner is showing you. Barbara Walters is famous for making her partners cry. The truth is she's not making them do anything. She's allowing them to experience honest emotions and sharing the experience. That's a true gift.

THE POWER OF WHY - EXPANDED

Celebrities have to answer the same questions repeatedly, and they often perfect some version of their answers in advance. They are also masters at deflecting anything they'd rather not discuss. So, how do you get something fresh? How do you get past the prepared talking points? How do you cut through the clutter and elicit a unique dialogue that stands out from the rest of the pack? Simple: *follow-up*.

The follow-up question may be the sharpest arrow in your quiver, and the shorter you can make it, the better. (I don't think that's actually true of arrows, but whatever.) As I mentioned, my favorite follow-up question is that little power-packed, three-letter gem: Why?

"*Why* do you say that?"

"*Why* did you make that choice?"

"*Why* does this character mean so much to you?"

You can pursue a subject more deeply by simply employing The Power of Why. Instead of letting her misdirect you into thinking, "I guess there's nothing there," simply follow-up with a quick: *What do you mean by that?* (a first cousin of why). Suddenly both of you are in uncharted waters where a real conversation can begin:

> KR: Was this a particularly difficult role?
>
> RENÉE ZELLWEGER: Oh, I had the best time playing this woman.
>
> KR: Really, why?
>
> RENÉE ZELLWEGER: Oh... well, because she's just so rigid. You know? And her expectations of people, and herself, are unrealistic. But at the same time, you know, she has to change her perspective a little bit and, and it's fun to watch her, you know, fail at trying to make the world do as she sees fit.

Your partner may give you subtle clues when you've triggered a rehearsed response. You'll know you've hit one of her talking points if she lapses into a singsong-y drone. She might sit back in her chair and exhale, indicating, "I can answer *this* without even thinking about it." That's OK. Let her get it out of the way. If treated correctly, the pat answer is the gatekeeper to the best information, but you have to pass through some doldrums to get there. *Why* is the path through and beyond.

When you've broken through a barrier, you'll know that too. Some indicators that you've hit pay dirt are if your partner…

- **Exhibits a burst of energy or volume**
- **Stammers slightly to find the right words.**
- **Shifts in her seat**
- **Widens her eyes and leans forward**
- **Inhales sharply and blurts out new information**

She may even contradict herself if a publicist or someone else gave her the rote answer to begin with. Or she might go off on a totally different tangent – let her. These reactions are the kind of awakening that you are hoping for: the good stuff behind the common response. Here's where you lean in and really start listening. The best material you'll get is on these tangents. When Hugh Jackman talked to me about his role in *Wolverine*, he touched on his daily preparation but then veered off. After he finished, I circled back:

> KR: You started to mention something that you did every morning of the shoot?
>
> HUGH JACKMAN: Did I? Oh, right. For Wolverine--he's a coiled spring. And I discovered, by accident, I was having a shower, there's no hot water, and I was in there and I - my wife is asleep so I couldn't yell or scream. And I - for

three minutes, stood under the coldest shower I've ever been in my life. ...You just wanna swear and yell, but you can't. I went... [stiffens] that's Wolverine all the time. So, every morning I would take a cold shower, when I played this role.

I had caught him editing himself but I didn't let it go. I'm glad I pursued it because no other interviewer had this tidbit. Unless it's truly some deep dark family secret (it isn't), this is the best material you'll get. Look for indications that there's more under the surface, then pursue it until you've uncovered the truth. The key is to lead your partner further down the road she's already on. That's *the power of why* in a nutshell – it opens closed doors.

AARON ECKHART: Burke [his character's name] has not healed and it takes Eloise to make that happen.

KR: Why?

AARON ECKHART: She's hot. [pause]

KR: [laughs] Ok, but what is it about her that heals him?

AARON ECKHART: Well, that's a good question. His life is not his own. You know? And so I think it would really take an intense connection for him to stop and look at a person and say, "You've affected me."

PERFECT THE PIVOT

Another skill that comes in handy is the ability to re-direct your partner when necessary. It's called *the pivot* because it's some fancy verbal footwork. It's not a total change in direction, rather a subtle course correction. It can be tricky but it's vital, especially if you have a limited amount of time (as in always).

Jon Voight told me five stories for each one I asked him about. Given his long history in the business, they were all fascinating, but I had a limited amount of time and had to rein him in. I wanted to keep him on my side, of course, so I phrased my pivot, "That's amazing and it makes me think of...[my original question]." Other phrases that work are, "How did that affect... [whatever you're supposed to be covering]," or the direct approach: "I'd love to hear more, but I have so little time..." Learn to do this politely so your partner doesn't feel like she's done something wrong. She'll get it if you're cool, and usually go where you lead.

INTENTIONAL INTERUPTIONS: THE EXCEPTION THAT PROVES THE RULE

Sometimes it's necessary to shake up the room. If you're heading down the wrong path or you feel like the interview is getting stiff or formal, break up the mood with a joke or sudden, unexpected comment. Interrupt your partner or even talk over her answer. This goes against what I've previously indicated, but it can be a helpful tool if used in moderation. Since this is such a cardinal sin, it usually has a big effect. Burst out laughing if she makes a joke, or make one yourself and watch all the tension in the room dissolve. If you're authentically amused, the crew may crack up too. This laugh probably won't make the final cut, but you've just made a solid connection and the cost is worth it. Plus, a big yuck from the crew is rare enough that sometimes it *does* make the cut.

You might want to purposely talk over your partner if:

- **The tone in the room is getting too serious**
- **You want her to loosen up and speak more freely**
- **You already have what you need and want a spontaneous reaction**

When I interviewed Sacha Baron Cohen for *Borat, Cultural Learnings of America For Make Benefit Glorious Nation of Kazakhstan* (Best. Title. Ever.), he did the entire interview in-character. Before I even started he reached out to shake my hand, but instead pulled me in and kissed me. Twice. Talk about shaking up the room. He caught me off guard and cracked up the whole set which changed the tone of my interview. The result: for the only time in my career, my client decided this piece would work better with me on-camera, so they paid me extra (as talent) and asked me to edit myself into the spot. Big Fun. Unique spot. And a couple extra bucks. Doesn't get more win-win than that!

Your larger goal is to create a bond and get honest, authentic answers. If that means going outside the usual boundaries occasionally, go for it. Just be aware you're doing it, and make sure you have the lines you need in the clear.

KEY TIP: NOTE TO SELF--MAKE NOTES TO YOURSELF

If your partner says something you need to remember or to look up after the interview, don't be afraid to jot down a quick note on your questions list. Do this discreetly, but don't worry if she sees you writing; it's part of your job. This is important because it's very hard to remember everything that was said after you've left the room.

This also includes subjects you want to bring up before you finish the interview. No one will mind if, at the end, you say, "Let me make sure I got everything," and check your notes.

CHAPTER EIGHT

WRAPPING IT UP AT THE JUNKET

YOUR LAST GOOD QUESTION

Wherever you are, whether it's a time-sensitive pressure cooker like a junket, or sitting with your partner in a more casual space, save an open-ended question for last. You're going to need a great ending for your piece. Bring your interview to a graceful end with a question like:

- What was the best part of this experience?
- What surprised you about the process?
- [Or even the direct:] Is there anything else you'd like to add?

The goal is to obtain a killer closing line like:

> **SWAMPY MARSH:**[7] **It's been magical. I don't want this to end. Can we do another one?**

For more examples, check out almost any *60 Minutes* segment. They always capture a salient button to sum up their point at the end. You should too.

KEY TIP: GET ONE LAST QUESTION IN UNDER THE WIRE.

To obtain that great button and extend your time at the junket, make your last question one that will take your partner some time to answer. The timekeepers will shut *you* down the second you go over, but they will never cut off the star. Toss off an open-ended query that lets your partner respond with a nice, long, well-considered answer like:

- **Why was this role important to you?**
- **What would you say to young ____s who want to do what you do?**
- **What was your favorite moment on the set?**

Your phrasing and tone signals to your partner that you're looking for some parting words. These will sound different than the rest of your interview.

---

[7] Yep, that's really his name.

KEY TIP: REMIND YOURSELF WHAT WAS SAID IMMEDIATELY AFTER YOUR INTERVIEW.

When your time is up, thank you partner, shake hands if appropriate, and exit quickly. After you leave, but before you hit the machine room for your media, jot down as many notes as you can from your interview. Junket interviews can be very rapid fire and, as the adrenaline subsides, so do the facts. This is especially true if you are interviewing more than one person in a day. Sometimes you'll be in a rotation and go from room to room and speak with half a dozen partners. They start to blend together, believe me, so while everything is still fresh, write down as much as you can, as soon as possible.

BEFORE YOU GO

When you're done taking notes, head down to the machine room. The team is busy so don't get in their way but they're expecting you to stop by and pick up your media. You can even request that they show you a short piece of your interview--just enough to make sure you've got the right one. This is not a question of their capabilities, just a double check--mistakes happen--and everyone wants to make sure any issues are caught as early as possible.

KEY TIP: GET TWO COPIES OF YOUR MEDIA.

Ask the technicians if you can have two copies of each card or drive with your media. You want two separate physical elements, not two versions of the media on the same card or drive. They usually don't mind. The advantages to this are:

- Cards/Drives get lost, and you want a back up for safety
- You might have to send a copy of the media to your client
- You can scan the media from your office without interrupting your editor
- You have the raw footage for the future in case you're creating a sizzle reel of your own. This is vital when bragging about all the cool people you've interviewed. Ok, I buried the lead – this last point is really the best reason for having your own copy of the media. You've got to promote yourself, right?

Once you've got your media, thank the staff and get out of there. These people have an exhausting day and will appreciate your being prompt, professional, polite and gone.

CHECKLIST: AT THE JUNKET

ON DECK

√ 3B's: Be on time. Be respectful. Be ready to go when called

√ Make friends with your nervous energy; if you don't have any – get some

√ Practice your questions while you're in a heightened state

IN THE ROOM

√ Start quickly

√ Ask your partner to incorporate your question into her answers

- √ Make a connection by treating her like a dear friend
- √ Get the Big Picture
- √ Listen Actively
- √ Edit in your head
- √ Authentic emotion *is* connection, don't shy away from it
- √ Paraphrase your questions – your list is just a guide
- √ Respond non-verbally to keep your audio clean
- √ Interrupt if you need to but don't overdo it
- √ Pivot when necessary
- √ Employ the Awesome Power of *Why?*
- √ Get a great closing line

BEFORE YOU GO

- √ Save an interesting, open-ended question for last
- √ Write a quick summary immediately after your interview.
- √ Get two copies of your media

PART TWO

IN YOUR OWN HOUSE

While the press junket is a unique animal with specific challenges and opportunities, it's not the only way to go. If you're in a position to produce your own shoot in a different location, congratulations. This freedom to flex your creative muscles is awesome and the spots you produce will stand out from the crowd because…

- **They will look different.** Everyone's junket interview looks the same because they're shot in the same room with the same ad art and the same celebrity wearing the same clothes.

- **They will sound different.** Since you aren't in the junket rotation with its inherent time constraints, you can set a more leisurely pace. This will be noticeable in your finished piece.

- **They will BE different.** With your own camera and sound crew, a different physical location, even different wardrobe your spots will be nothing like the rest of the pack.

The range of options you have in this situation is both exhilarating and daunting at the same time. When you're at a junket, you're treated almost as a guest. When you shoot in your own location, you're the director. Enjoy the experience and make the most of this opportunity.

TREAT YOUR CREW LIKE GOLD

Start your day by briefing everyone on your creative vision. Have a short company meeting early, go over your plan for the day and respond to any questions. Professional crews are used to working with very little information, but the more you can give them, the better. Tell them what you want to achieve, but don't tell them how to do it. Let them figure out how to support your vision themselves--that's a big part of what makes their jobs fun. Plan to have nothing left to do about five minutes before your deadline. Then find one more thing to do.

Golden Rules all around: "please and thank you" go a long way, and *never* yell at a crewmember, especially in front of anyone else. You want a room full of good vibes so keep the energy light, stay on task, find things to laugh at and watch the clock.

LEGAL - EASE

Don't forget the releases! Whenever you put someone on-camera, make sure you're covered legally by asking her to sign an Appearance Release. It's a one-page, boilerplate, legal document that allows you to use her likeness and views on-air, on the web or (hold onto something): "in whole or in part, in any manner whatsoever, by any and all means, media, devices, processes and technology now or hereafter known or devised *in perpetuity throughout the universe.*" That ought to cover it. Sure, this sounds like the demands of a super villain, but it has become pretty standard in the entertainment industry. It is aimed at retaining the rights to your interview even as technology changes. It is also why a well-known actor once took one look at that phrase, read it out loud to me with a sneer, and ripped the document in half. Slowly. I got the message. I wouldn't be filming him that day. Still, ask them to sign. Most of them will, and it's another layer of protection for you and your client. This is handled for you at a junket by the studio, but when you produce your own shoot, it's your responsibility.

You may also need a Location Release. This should be signed by the owner of the property or her agent and allows you to air identifiable sections of the environment. As above, this is not always necessary, but nice to have if you're shooting in a public location. In which case you would also be wise to print some poster-sized copies of a Notice of Public Filming And Consent Release. Mount this blown-up document on foam core or stiff cardboard and post it in at least two entrances/exits to your location, then film the signs with people walking by. This is to make sure the public is aware that they may be filmed and shown on air. You want to be able to prove that you notified everyone in advance.

There are exceptions, of course. Not everyone needs to sign a release. Many actors are doing interviews as part of their contractual promotional duties, so they've already signed blanket releases that cover press. If you're the least bit in doubt, ask their handlers. There's no point getting bogged down in paperwork if you don't have to. But if you do, leave a copy of the release on your partner's chair so she can't fail to see it and, get it out of the way.

Like many legal documents, you'll probably file these away and never look at them again. If anything comes up, however, it's great to be able to show that you got permission. Your client's Legal Department will thank you for it.

But where are you supposed to find these release? Good Question! Ask your client if her legal department has any preferred forms or language. If not, generic versions of these releases can be found and downloaded from: GoodQuestionTheBook.com. Don't mention it.

CHAPTER NINE

SETTING UP YOUR SHOT

I f you conducted a scout, you should already know the dimensions and physical attributes of your location. If not, it will be the first thing on your agenda the day of the shoot. In most cases, you will only have a single person on-camera, so you only need to set up one area. If, however, you are going to be on-camera as well, you'll need a different configuration. Below I've described the most common variations in detail.

The usual set-up is one person on-camera (your partner) and one person (you) asking questions from off-camera. Your three main decisions, then, are:

- **Where do you want your partner?**
- **Where do you want yourself?**
- **Where do you want the camera?**

WHERE DO YOU WANT YOUR PARTNER?

The room itself will often dictate the best position for your partner so let geography be your guide. Each room will present different pros and cons, but for a single interview, you only need enough room for the camera and lights, an attractive or neutral background and some separation from the wall. Compose the shot as if you were taking a photograph. Focus on simplicity, balance and visual interest with a minimum of distractions.

Place your partner where she is facing the camera, slightly to one side of the frame, and with her face turned toward the other side. For example, frame her slightly to the left of frame, looking to the camera right, or vice versa. Work with your DP and Art Director to create a physical set and lights to achieve this. Usually this is a case of *less is more*. With a little practice, you'll know when it feels right. Trust your instincts and get used to taking advice from your team. Get everything the way you like it, then show it to the client for sign-off and/or notes.

Here are things to consider:

- **Are the existing walls useful for your look?**
- **If not, can you add a backdrop or other replacement?**
- **Do you want any ad art in the shot such as posters or props from the movie?**
- **How about some flowers? A little bit of color is nice, but you don't want a jungle.**
- **Are you bringing in furniture? A rug? Wall units? Lamps, etc.?**

You can create almost any set with enough time and money, but keep in mind that your main subject is always your partner. Keep her front and center (well, slightly off-center). Once you've established the look of your set, let the DP and Gaffer light it, and watch as your concept goes from good to great. That's just what these people do.

KEY TIP: ALWAYS USE TWO <u>MATCHED</u> CHAIRS THAT DON'T SWIVEL.

The style and size of the chairs you choose for your interview is limited only to your imagination. Make sure to use a pair of identical chairs, even though one of them–yours–will never be seen. This ensures a perfect eye-line for your partner because two matching chairs will always be exactly the same height. I keep some nice counter stools--slightly lower than barstools--with padded seats that I've used dozens of times. They're simple, they're virtually hidden on camera, and they don't swivel!

PROS AND CONS OF DIRECTOR'S CHAIRS

Director's chairs are the go-to seating on most film sets. They fit easily in a car and raise your partner up high enough to keep your DP happy (it's easier to shoot someone who's above chair level). They're readily available and a simple solution for a quick set-up. If you're in a rush or on a limited budget, director's chairs are fine. For interviews, however, they do have some disadvantages.

For one thing, unless they're brand new, they're not very stable so they tend to move around. Older ones creak like Boston Whalers. They have no back support so they cause people to slouch and reposition themselves repeatedly. The arms are slightly higher than normal chairs and this hunches up your partner's shoulders. And then there are those pesky little wooden posts that hold up the canvas back. To some, this is the most aggravating aspect of all. These little devils can peek up over your partner's shoulders in a distracting way. I had a client point this out to me once and there was no way to fix it until we changed chairs. Solve the problem before it begins and avoid director's chairs if you can.

KEY TIP: IS SOMETHING GROWING OUT OF YOUR PARTNER'S HEAD?

When you're in a practical location[8] you will often have to make do with design elements you can't change. This includes furniture, wallpaper, windows and other physical elements of your environment. Make sure, therefore, that there are no vertical lines directly behind your partner. Don't put her in front of a lamp, a doorjamb or a plant or it will appear to be coming straight out of her head. Move it, or her, as soon as you notice this. Same goes for pillars, wall molding, trees—you get the picture. You might not notice it immediately with the naked eye because we're used to subconsciously editing out background elements in real life, so check your shot on the monitor. Suddenly these elements become glaringly apparent.

Go easy on this, however; you can over-worry about it. Something in the distance that's in soft focus is not going to cause a problem. It's more of a guideline than a hard and fast rule.

KEY TIP: WATCH WINDOWS IN YOUR SHOT.

A downtown skyline or a bucolic landscape can be an incredibly beautiful backdrop for any shoot. A talented DP can make

---

[8] An area used for another purpose when you're not there, such as a living room, a restaurant, hotel room, etc.

this work, and larger productions often tint the window glass or even fake the background entirely. In an interview setting, however, you may not have that kind of time and control, and windows can present a number of challenges.

The natural light coming through a real window is usually too bright for your camera, and may cause your shot to "blow out" into a glaring white blob. You can mitigate the glare by covering the glass with a sheet of ND[9] which your DP or Art Director can rig. Also, throughout the day the sun will move, so if you're shooting for more than about fifteen minutes, your lighting will change from the beginning to the end of your interview. ND-ing the window can be time consuming, however, so it is best to avoid windows altogether. If in doubt, save yourself some headaches and aim your camera elsewhere.

WHERE ARE YOU? THE INTERVIEWER'S CHAIR

This is probably the easiest decision you'll make because in most of your interviews you'll be off-camera, not in the shot. Therefore, as soon as your partner's position is locked, set your chair right next to the camera's lens. Get as close to your partner as you can without entering the shot, and as close to the lens without bumping it. Your chair should go on the <u>same side of the lens as the key light</u> - your partner's primary front light (see Fig. A).

---

[9] "Neutral Density" - a sheet of plastic or gel that creates temporarily tinted windows.

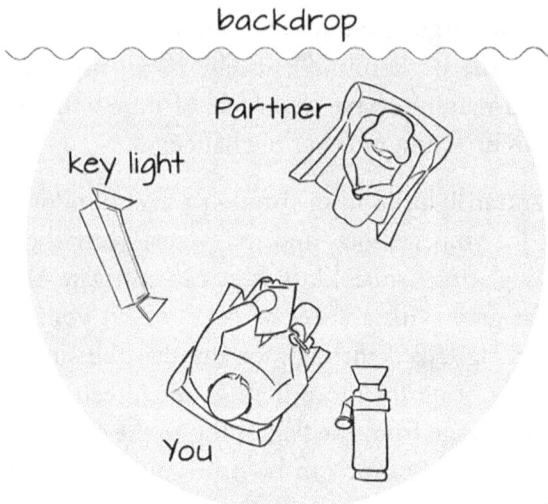

Fig. A. Your chair is on the same side of the camera as the key light

KEY TIP: FLOP THE KEY

If you're interviewing more than one partner and they will all appear in the final piece, I strongly recommend that you "flop the key" for half of your interviews. Simply move the key light to the other side of the camera, and reposition your chair on that side as well. This will give your final spot some welcome variety as half of our partners will be looking in to the other side of the frame.

RIGHT DOWN THE PIPE

Setting your chair right up against the camera gives your interview a traditional look, but there is an alternative. With the proliferation of selfies, VLOGs, how-to videos and user generated content (UGC), a new trend has emerged that offers another option. Your partner can speak directly *into* the camera without loosing contact with you.

There are various ways of achieving this. The preferred method was developed by documentary filmmaker, Errol Morris. He calls it the *Interrotron* and uses a pair of specially rigged teleprompters to feed live images of himself and his partner "into" each camera. This allows him and his partner to see each other while looking right into the lens. This technique creates an intimate, almost "first person" feeling to an interview and is especially effective with emotionally charged subjects.

Another simpler approach is to use a device called *EyeDirect* which uses a series of mirrors, almost like a periscope, instead of teleprompters. Either way, the result looks like a Skype connection and offers an alternative to the traditional interview paradigm.

CHAPTER TEN

CAMERA PLACEMENT

W hole sections of film libraries have been devoted to the placement of the camera. Where you want your camera is about as simple a decision as, "What do you want to paint?" Since we're concentrating on a specific kind of shot in a unique world, I'm going to keep this accordingly direct. You can get as artsy as you want with dollies, Steadicams, drones, whatever; but first learn the basics. Then, go nuts. Even before that, however, let's clear away an obstacle that has tripped up directors young and old for years.

THE 180° RULE DEMYSTIFIED

For those who have already mastered this concept, feel free to skip ahead. For those new to production, however, this is one of the pesky little items that comes up repeatedly and is debated from commercial shoots to features. The "180° Rule" is an imaginary boundary that your cameras *cannot* cross under any circumstances… unless you feel like it.[10] It seems counter-intuitive, arbitrary and slightly baffling but, if you unpack it, it's not that hard to master. I finally sat down with a patient DP and he gave me the simple version; best five minutes of my career. I'm about to save you all that time. Think nothing of it.

The purpose of the 180° rule is to make sure everyone is looking in the right direction. For example, if you and your partner are both on-camera, you will be framed slightly off center to the right, your eyes looking *camera left*. You will appear to be facing the left side of the screen. Your partner, then, should be framed the opposite way: slightly off center to the left, looking *camera right* so it appears as if you're looking at each other.[11] Simple enough, right? To achieve this, however, the camera positions are *not* mirrors of each other as you'd expect. They have to be on the same side of the 180° line.

As you and your partner face each other, draw an imaginary line between the tips of your noses. Extend the line through and beyond each of your heads as if you'd both been skewered by the same thirty-foot (imaginary) sword. Now picture an arc or semi circle extending towards the camera, from the point of the sword all the way around to the handle. The sword's blade is the line you can't cross; the arc is where you can place your camera(s). (See Fig. B).

---

[10] There are cases where it's appropriate and I mention those at the end of this chapter. Stick around, they're cool.

[11] Camera Right & Camera Left are easy, they're the viewers' right or left while looking at the screen. It's the exact opposite of Stage Right & Stage Left, which are from the perspective of a live performer facing the audience. On a film set, only the former is used.

GOOD QUESTION!

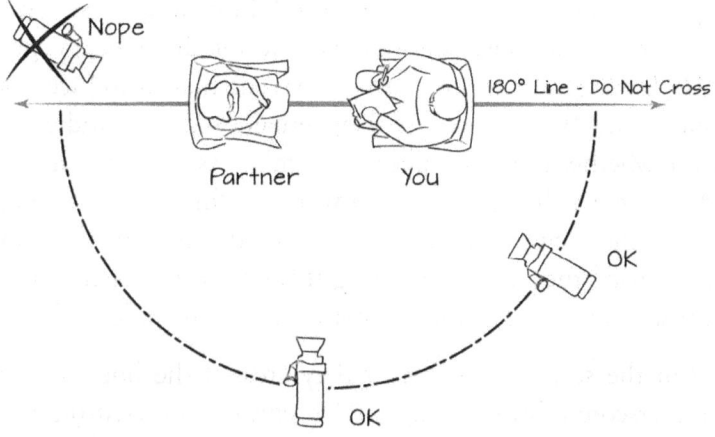

Fig. B. Correct camera positions on one side of the 180° Line

This is essential so that the viewers understand the geography of the scene. Your DP is the first person to ask for help achieving this. If you're lucky enough to have a Script Supervisor (commonly nicknamed Scripty,) it's actually part of her job to ensure you never cross the line. Between the three of you (and everyone else who went to film school), you should be able to nail this. If you don't, it's sometimes fixable in post by flopping a shot (reversing it horizontally) but try and avoid that by shooting it correctly in the first place.

KEY TIP: WHEN TO BREAK THE 180° RULE.

Like many rules, this one was made to be broken. Crossing the line can disorient the audience, so if you want to intentionally mess with the viewer, say in a horror film or a tense, dramatic sequence, you might choose to cross the line on purpose. It's a subtle, almost unconscious signal to your viewer that something is fundamentally askew.

The legendary director John Ford did this when it suited his purposes. He famously crossed the line for dramatic purposes in *My Darling Clementine* during the scene that introduces Doc Holiday and Wyatt Earp. As they verbally spar, the audience is unsure whether they'll be allies or enemies. As the threat mounts and the power shifts, the camera work reinforces the tension by keeping the viewer off-balance. I counted four different times Ford crossed the 180° line during this one scene, each time on purpose. Subtle and brilliant. That's a master at work.

On the series *In Treatment* they crossed the line routinely to underscore a breakthrough. Each episode centered on a different therapy session, so the 180° line was well-established as the patient and therapist faced each other. Often about half way through the narrative, just as a moment of clarity was achieved, the camera would drift to the other side of the line, subtly reinforcing this change in perception.

Sadly, that kind of opportunity rarely comes up in interviews. It's usually restricted to narrative pieces where the director's goal is to make the audience uneasy or scared. (Wait, Horror Interviews! Did I just invent a new genre?) Bottom line: learn the rule before you break it.

WHERE TO PUT YOUR CAMERA(S)

How many cameras you have will dictate where you put them, of course. Below are some options with which you can make informed decisions about their placement. Start by requesting as many cameras as you need. Your client will always rein you in with budgetary or other restrictions but you never know; she might actually say yes. This year was the first time I ever asked for a full-sized crane on a shoot, and I got it! *Fortune favors the bold,* as they say, so don't be afraid to request big even if you often have to settle for less.

ONE PERSON / ONE CAMERA

The smallest crew you can get away with is three people: one camera person, one sound person and one producer/interviewer. This is often referred to as an ENG crew, an old term still in use that stands for Electronic News Gathering. It references the three-man crews local stations send out when news breaks. It makes sense in cases like red carpet events or where there's very little room, extremely low budgets, etc. Don't be surprised if you have to make do under these circumstances occasionally. And don't get me wrong, ENG crews can yield very good results. They usually fit into the run-and-gun category where you have to get in, do the job and get out quickly, as the name implies. If you have some time, some luck and some experience you can set up and shoot a nice looking interview. Still, I advise that you request a more substantial crew whenever possible.

ONE PERSON / TWO CAMERAS

One of the best ways to add production value to your one-person interview is to use two cameras. Even though your partner will be the only one on-camera, a second camera gives you a second angle and a number of additional options. The second or *B Camera* can be positioned either shoulder-to-shoulder with your *A Camera*, or further to one side for a more dramatic profile.

For variety, make sure and frame your B Camera differently than A Camera, either slightly wider or more of a CU. The different sizes will give dimension and visual interest to your piece.

Plus this second angle will allow you to edit in the middle of a sentence for dramatic or narrative effect. And maybe best of all, a second angle frees you up in post to do pull-ups as needed.[12] Consequently it's well worth asking for a second camera in your budget talks.

TWO PEOPLE / TWO CAMERAS

If you are going to be on-camera yourself along with your partner, the minimum you'll need is two cameras. This is how most junkets are staged, providing a Medium Over of both you and your partner. This gives the coverage you need and is easy to set up. It leaves you without a Wide or 2-Shot unfortunately, but sometimes that's the best you can do.

First set up your partner's shot exactly the same way you would with only one camera, except that it will be over your shoulder, a shot not surprisingly referred to as an *Over*. Then set up *your* shot over your partner's shoulder. Both Overs should be Medium Close-ups, but you can choose to compose them in one of two ways: "clean or dirty." A Clean Over means there's nothing else in the shot but you. A Dirty Over includes a piece or your partner's shoulder in the foreground, usually in soft-focus. Clean is best for interviews unless you're after a unique look. Dirty Overs are traditionally used in narrative pieces, but either will work so it's your call.

ADDING A THIRD CAMERA

If you can acquire three cameras for your shoot you're in great shape. Now you can capture a Master (Wide Shot) while the A

---

[12] A pull-up is a term for shortening a line by editing out words or pauses from the middle of it.

& B Cameras get your Close-ups. There are so many advantages to this set-up that you should try and persuade your client to spring for it whenever possible. Regale her with the virtues of this model including:

- **A wonderful opening and closing Wide Shot**
- **An uninterrupted flow to the interview**
- **A less claustrophobic feel to the viewer**
- **More options in post**

There are many options for camera placement, but this is the basic set-up (See Fig. C).

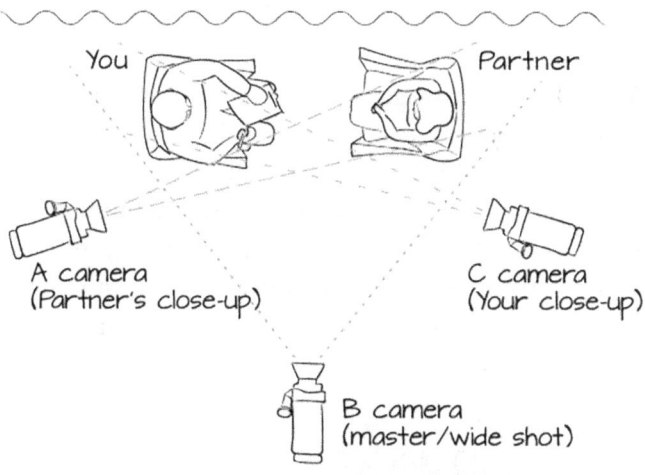

Fig. C. Three-camera set-up for two people on-camera

Fig. C features two subjects: you in the left chair, your partner in the right. *A Camera* is behind you, shooting your partner's

Over. *C Camera* is behind your partner, shooting your Over. And *B Camera* is right in the middle capturing your Master or Wide Shot.

If you only have two cameras and two people to cover, it's best to devote one camera to the Wide, and the other to "chasing singles." That means panning back and forth between speakers. As you can imagine, this is a dicey proposition, but not unheard of in these budget-conscious times.

On the other hand, if you have an unlimited budget (it could happen), go with the *60 Minutes* model and place *four* cameras in the room: one for each Over, one for the Wide Shot and one additional Close-up of your partner. That makes three angles on your partner and two on you (the Wide Shot includes both of you), and your editor will be spoiled for choice.

This also gives you coverage in case there are any surprises. If someone tears up or struggles for the answer to a tough question, your Close-up camera is already in position and doesn't have to zoom in suddenly. Bill and Hillary Clinton were in the middle of an interview when a light suddenly fell and almost hit them. The various cameras were in position to catch their reactions and the whole startling event. Maybe not the cheeriest example, but it does prove the point: the more cameras you have, the more you're prepared for.

KEEP THE CAMERA MOVING

Adding a slight *drift* to the camera all the way through your interview looks great. I know a studio executive that jokingly remarks his only purpose on a set is to make sure they keep the camera moving. Movement adds life to your shot that you don't get with a Lock-Off, and makes everything look more fluid. If I can only one drift one camera, I usually choose the one capturing my Wide Shot as it makes the move more noticeable (See Fig. C again). That said, a little drift looks great on the Close-up Cameras as well. Okay, it looks great everywhere.

There are a number of ways to add movement to your camera. You can use a dolly, a Stedicam, a jib, a GoPro, even a drone if you're adventurous. My preference is a small piece of hardware called a slider. It looks like a long metal tray that fits between the camera and the tripod, sticking out on both sides like wings. The whole thing is usually between three and six feet long and allows the camera to slide gracefully over that distance. The Camera Operator pulls the camera manually during the shot, and the effect is a smooth, gradual drift that gives you a subtle and elegant look.

To really kick it up a notch, get multiple sliders and put one on each camera. Just make sure to discuss this in advance with your crew. They may not have the equipment with them if you come up with this idea on the shoot day.

OR "SET IT AND FORGET IT"

There is, of course, an alternative to a drifting shot. You don't get the same production value, but it's better than nothing and it will save you so much money that it's worth considering. You can position one camera on a tripod to capture your Wide Shot, then lock it off and just "set it and forget it." Just set your frame, tighten down the screws and let it run without an operator. This provides you with a static Wide Shot and saves you money since you only need the additional camera without the additional crewmember. It's not my favorite option, but it's better than only two cameras, so don't be afraid to use it if nothing else is available.

CHAPTER ELEVEN

TOPS AND TAILS

NEVER MAKE YOUR PARTNER WAIT

Once you and your client are happy with your shot, get ready for your partner so you can start rolling as soon as she arrives. I have one client who cares more about this directive than almost any other aspect of production. "Content is king," he admits, "but if you *ever* make the celebrity wait, you're fired." I think he's kidding, but I've never tested my theory.

Minutes before your partner's arrival do a final idiot check. Make sure all the elements in the room are where you want them. Look around her position at everything else in the shot. Verify that there are no dead flowers in the vase, no glare coming off a background element, no boom in the shot, etc. Have someone sit in your partner's position and check again. Ask if each department has everything they need. And if everyone is totally ready, tidy up.

DON'T SKIP THE DRESS REHEARSAL

If you still have a few minutes, run a dress rehearsal: a logistical run-through of everything you expect to happen. Have a stand-in enter the room as the talent. Decide who greets her first, you or the client? Where does she go, right to the chair or into hair/make-up? Is there a clear path to her chair with all the cables dressed (taped down)? Consider this exercise successful if you discover something that needs fixing.

KEY TIP: FIND OUT WHAT YOUR PARTNER LIKES AND SUPPLY IT.

If possible, provide your partner with something unique that she enjoys. Jennifer Love-Hewitt is a devoted *Journey* fan. You can bet we had their Greatest Hits pumping when she entered the room. Ron Perlman of *Sons of Anarchy* and *Hell Boy* fame kept a tiny dog with him during the whole interview. We had a water bowl. If nothing else, always have a open bottle of water near your partner's chair. And if your partner is a woman, make sure you include a bendy straw in it to avoid smearing her lipstick.

ARRIVALS

Celebrities have tremendous demands on their time, so be considerate of her schedule. Once she arrives, introduce yourself, your crew, the DP and the Sound person. Many people forget about Sound, but this technician will be attaching a mic to your partner's clothes so it's best if they've met.

Walk your partner to her chair, tell her what you plan to do and how long you expect it to take. Double check if she has any time constraints you should be aware of. Invite her team to look at the monitor so they can sign off on the shot. Then, the only waiting she should experience is the time it takes to answer any questions, and for you to call:

"LAST LOOKS!"

This is the cue for your team to execute any final tweaks to the set, lighting or sound. Win over your partner's glam squad (hair/make-up) by learning their names and letting them step in before you start. Too many directors treat these talented artists as a nuisance and that's a mistake. You are all working toward the same goal so encourage them to contribute.

Once all teams are ready, dive in. Everyone has a schedule to keep and the sooner you start, ...y'know. Once everyone is in position, say a polite but assertive "Very quiet please," and instruct your DP to roll if she hasn't already. As soon as you hear that camera and sound are both speeding, start your questions.

Once you start your interview, all the same guidelines apply that I've enumerated in Chapters Five through Eight. The only differences between an interview at a junket and one you set up yourself are at the beginning and the end of the process. I've already covered the beginning—your preparation and the set-up of the shot. Now here are some tips to get you out the door with everything you need.

CHECK IN WITH YOUR CLIENT

Make sure your client is happy as often as feasible. You don't want to get up and leave your chair if you don't have to, so it's helpful to station her where you can see her during the interview. Check in with her before you end the interview and ask if she feels you've gotten everything you need. This extra consideration is not only polite, it ensures that no one can say later, "I wish you had asked…" Then, once you know you're golden:

DON'T CUT OFF THE HANDLES

Give your editor the tools she needs by providing *handles* during the shoot. This is what editors call the pauses before and after a line that allow them to fade out, swell the music or transition to another shot without any *lip flap* (a talking head without sound). You want a little silence after your favorite lines so, when you know you're done with your interview, lock eyes, hold your breath and *don't say, "Cut" until you've silently counted to three.* Sometimes I even raise my hand like a conductor coming to a downbeat, count to three in my head, and then bring it down saying, "…aaaaand cut." This causes my partner to stare at me like I'm nuts, without speaking, and that gives me the handles I need.

ROOM TONE

When you've finished your interview, but before you wrap any equipment, this is the very last thing you'll want to shoot. There is some debate over the usefulness of this slightly old-school practice, but if anything even *might* give you an advantage in post, I say use it. Room tone is one of those advantages. It simply means recording about thirty seconds of absolute silence while the room is still full of people. The value of this is in post-production. When you start editing, there's a good chance you'll need to massage some of your partner's responses. To do it seamlessly, you'll want some air between the edits to ensure it sounds like natural speech. Room tone is the element you'll need to make this work. Just leaving a gap devoid of sound between edits is noticeable, so providing a few seconds of ambient silence will help a lot.

Most people get room tone at the end of their shoots, and if that's your only option, by all means do it. Release your partner, clear the room of anyone who needs to go (but not everyone; you don't want an empty room) and lock down the set. Say a quick, "Everyone please freeze for thirty seconds of room tone," and roll both camera and sound. This is primarily an audio element but it's helpful to shoot it as well, so aim the camera at something innocuous but indicative like a microphone, the boom or the slate just so it's easy for your editor to find.

Expert audio mixer Tony Friedman suggests one more thing to give you an additional edge. He encourages that you to get room tone *first*, not last. If you have time to grab tone before you start your interview, you gain a number of additional benefits including:

- **You verify that the audio is actually being recorded**
- **You identify or rule out any buzz from the cables, or battery issues**
- **You correct any issues, audio or otherwise, before wasting your partner's time**
- **Oh, and you get room tone.**

I don't recommend keeping your partner around for Room Tone. Even though it would give you the *absolutely* best audio match, it's a little weird to ask a celebrity to sit tight for such a technical element. Let her go after the interview and then get tone, or capture it before she arrives if you have time.

KEY TIP: THEN LISTEN BACK TO YOUR AUDIO IN A DIFFERENT ROOM.

Here's Tony again advising how to verify you have what you need:

Listen back on headphones in another space. In the room, your brain will trick you by allowing you to mentally filter out extraneous noise—air conditioning, street noise, etc.—playback through headphones will not. Once you take yourself out of the space and listen on headphones, your brain gets out of the way and you hear what is really being recorded.

TAIL LIGHTS

Make sure to restore your location to its original state before you go. This is when those photos you took at the scout come in handy. After your team has packed up and loaded out, use those pictures and walk around the space. Ask your location contact to sign off before you go. This is one of the most common mistakes made by small film crews – leaving a mess in their wake. Make sure you're invited back by cleaning up after yourself.

CHECKLIST: IN YOUR OWN HOUSE

SETTING UP THE SHOT

- √ Treat your crew like gold
- √ Bring the releases you need
- √ Decide where you want your partner and yourself
- √ Beware of:
  - > Director's chairs
  - > Windows
  - > Things coming out of your partner's head
- √ Decide where you want your camera(s) based on how many you have
- √ Flop the key for half your interviews if you have more than one
- √ Keep the camera moving
- √ Or don't

PRE-ARRIVAL OF YOUR PARTNER

- √ Be ready early!
- √ Conduct a dress rehearsal if you have time
- √ Get client approval of your shot
- √ Ensure the A/C is off or can be turned off (can take a few minutes to cycle)
- √ Stow all gear neatly and/or out of sight

- √ Phones on stun
- √ Clear the path from the door to your partner's chair
- √ Place an open bottle of water with a straw within reach of her chair
- √ Leave the talent release, if necessary, and a pen on her chair
- √ Capture thirty seconds of room tone before you start if possible

ARRIVAL

- √ Introduce yourself and your crew to your partner
- √ Show her to her chair and tell her what to expect
- √ Show her team the shot you're planning on the monitor
- √ Learn the names of the glam squad and let them contribute
- √ Call Last Looks and do final tweaks
- √ Follow the rules of a great interview from Chapter Eight:
  - › Start quickly
  - › Ask your partner to incorporate your question into her answers
  - › Make a connection by treating her like a dear friend
  - › Get the Big Picture
  - › Listen Actively
  - › Edit in your head
  - › Authentic emotion is connection, don't shy away from it
  - › Paraphrase your questions – your list is just a guide
  - › Respond non-verbally to keep your audio clean

> Interrupt if you need to but don't overdo it
> Pivot when necessary
> Employ the Awesome Power of WHY?
> Get a great closing line

BEFORE YOU GO

√ Check in with client often
√ Get Handles by silently counting to three before saying Cut
√ Release your partner and team
√ Record room tone if you haven't already
√ Restore the room to its pristine condition

CHAPTER TWELVE

BEST-LAID PLANS

WHAT COULD GO WRONG?

There will always be surprises. Some will be insignificant, some insurmountable and all unpredictable. No matter how well prepared you are you can still be blind-sided. For one thing, everything could go swimmingly – that *would* be a surprise. Or you could be caught flat-footed by something out of the clear blue. Hopefully you can correct it but sometimes, all you can do is roll with it.

I once directed Hollywood icon Robert Wagner for some movie wraparounds--intros and outros that bookended some re-discovered movies. My team and I took extra pains to ensure that we were ready on all fronts. I could have sworn I had told the crew, "phones on stun", but right in the middle of a take someone's mobile rang! RJ (as he is known) was ready to spit nails—until he realized it was his own phone. He calmed down quickly, and, in fact, took the call. It was his wife. They chatted about dinner, but he had to go. He told me afterward, "Never apologize. That's what they teach you in 'star school.'" We laughed it off and got back to work but it would have gone very differently if it had been *my* phone ruining the take.

When Sir Anthony Hopkins was promoting his film *The Rite* in Mexico, a respected journalist by the name of Joaquín López Dóriga interviewed him. Unfortunately, Dóriga doesn't speak English, and Hopkins doesn't speak Spanish. To overcome this minor hurdle, the producers gave Sir Anthony an earpiece with a translator as if he were at the UN. What happened next became a meme so popular it may never leave YouTube. At last count it had dozens of *millions* of views.

The hiccup was simple – the earpiece didn't work and the interview was live. After a couple of questions that Hopkins couldn't understand, he tapped his earpiece to indicate that he wasn't getting anything. The two tried their best to communicate in variations of Span-glish but to no avail. So Dóriga made one last valiant attempt with the little English he could muster.

He meant to say something to the effect of "Why did you do this film, The Rite?" which, in Spanish is called *El Rito*. He managed to combine the two languages in three words with a heavily accented, "Why The Rito?" Sir Anthony looked like he'd been pole-axed. He struggled to understand, finally gleaning, "Oh, *The Rite*, Why?" He gave a nice answer about liking the script, etc., but the initial awkwardness struck a nerve with the audience. Viewers took hold of this small moment, spelled it phonetically in Spanish as "Juay De Rito?" and posted it over and over again for everyone's amusement. At last count, Google-ing *Juay De Rito* resulted in 20,500 posts, including dozens of re-cuts and musical mash-ups. It even has its own Facebook page! No real harm done, of course, but a perfect example of the unpredictability of this medium. On the flip side, the film made close to five times its projected box office in Mexico due to the notoriety of this viral snafu. Chalk one up to the profitability of unintended consequences.

THE OTHER SIDE OF HAPPENSTANCE

You also never know when something will go incredibly *right*. Be prepared to take advantage of whatever comes your way. I once directed Justin Timberlake to appear as if he were on one end of a Skype-like interaction. I explained to him what I was after, had his script on the teleprompter and got ready to read the other half of the dialogue to cue him. Then, just before we started rolling, his team informed me that I only got one take. Oh…OK.

Fortunately Justin is terrific and charming and his performance was spot on, but I needed a couple of options on the way he said the title of the movie. I couldn't stop and ask for another take so when he got to the title I interrupted with, "I'm sorry, I rustled my papers over that last bit; can you pick it up from a line before?" He didn't mind, and his team couldn't complain.

Then, when he'd finished, I counted to three in my head and was about to say, "….aaaand c--" when he suddenly announced, "I think we kind of Nailed That!" Glorious. I had him saying a line no one expected which I was able to use to great effect. Bottom line: be alert for surprises, good or bad, and use everything you can.

Of course, you can't always protect yourself. Sometimes you'll get terse or even one-word answers no matter how open-ended your questions. I've walked into more than a few bad moods that had nothing to do with me. Sometimes my partner warmed up, sometimes not. Hopefully you can salvage a less-than-ideal situation. That is, unless you are faced with the worst possible situation: a partner who doesn't want to be there *at all*. Case in point:

PAINFULLY AWKWARD MINUTES

Sometimes, no matter what you do, the situation is impossible to save. To illustrate this unique slice of Hell, let me direct you to the clip I mentioned earlier: *7 Painfully Awkward Minutes with Jerry Lewis.*

Andy Lewis from The Hollywood Reporter (no relation to Jerry) unwittingly walked into this ninety-one year old buzz saw. He commented later that the iconic comedian was getting more and more frustrated as the camera and equipment were being set up and, "seemed like he was punishing The Hollywood Reporter by being as uncooperative as possible."

With admirable humility, Andy posted his entire interview online, un-cut so you can hear the whole thing in all its cringe-worthy glory. It's a cautionary tale, as well as a variation on the old adage: when life gives you lemons…well, just hope you like lemons.

It all started innocently enough with what seemed like a softball question:

> **ANDY LEWIS:** We're doing a feature on people who are still working in their 90's. Have you ever thought about retiring?
>
> **JERRY LEWIS** [belligerently]: Why?

> ANDY LEWIS: Uh... was there never a moment when you thought it might be time to retire or you would want--
>
> JERRY LEWIS [louder]: WHY?

Uh oh. Soldiering on...

> ANDY LEWIS: You come from a generation, a little older, I think of Bob Hope, George Burns, Sinatra—people you knew. Many of whom didn't want to—or never retired either. Do you see similarities with them?
>
> JERRY LEWIS: None.

Admittedly that was a long run up to a question, and Jerry took the easy way out by just answering the last part. Plus, he was in a mood. A little later:

> ANDY LEWIS: You've had a number of health issues over the last few years—
>
> JERRY LEWIS: Anyone who's 90 does.
>
> ANDY LEWIS: Does continuing to work—does that actually help you get healthier? You know, does being sort of busy and engaged, do you think that actually helps you get healthier?
>
> JERRY LEWIS: No.

Poor Andy Lewis was being buried, stone by stone, by the dreaded one-word answer.

KEY TIP: BE ON THE LOOKOUT FOR LIFE PRESERVERS

At one point, Jerry seemed to thaw for a moment on the subject of his late partner, Dean Martin. That might have been a route to calmer waters if Andy had stayed on that tack a little longer. Not all life preservers will save you, but any port in a storm to extend the metaphor. Also notice one of the many things that Andy Lewis did exactly right: he was extremely well informed about his partner's work. When he referenced Jerry Lewis' latest project, the comedian immediately challenged him:

> ANDY LEWIS: You just did a movie a couple years ago that's coming out--
>
> JERRY LEWIS (pouncing): What movie?
>
> ANDY LEWIS: Max Rose, right?
>
> JERRY LEWIS: (relaxing) I'm glad you remembered it.

It really looked like Jerry could have ended the interview right there if Andy Lewis had hesitated, but he's a pro. Sometimes the most you can hope for is to find *any* moments you can salvage. Uncover something your partner enjoys and stay on that subject as long as you can. Maybe make him laugh by asking, "What do you like to do on your days off, besides giving interviews, of course?" Let him vent if that's what it takes, but try and connect the way you would with anyone you really want to get to know. Keep it light, hope for the best, and don't beat yourself up if you hit a brick wall.

With any luck, this will be a rare occurrence, and who knows - maybe you can post a video of it like Andy Lewis did. That's turning lemons into lemonade, digital style.

Section Three

 # POST-PRODUCTION

PUTTING IT TOGETHER

CHAPTER THIRTEEN

PREPPING FOR YOUR EDITOR

YOUR NEW TEAM

Many people consider post-production the most satisfying part of the whole process, and I can see why. When you are editing, mixing and finishing your spot, all your work comes together into one cohesive whole. You get to work with a totally different team of artists and technicians who command incredibly powerful, high-tech tools. What's not to love?

Editors, graphic designers, sound mixers and other post-production professionals are some of the smartest, funniest, most creative people in the business. Keep in mind that they spend most of their time in dark rooms, alone, creating silk purses out of—well, lots of things. Give them a little latitude if they seem eccentric.

Your post team is usually facing an unforgiving schedule, so they're used to making decisions quickly. Help them out by following suit. They might try and restrain you with the old saw, "How do you want this project; great, fast or cheap? Pick two." The truth is they're used to delivering all three. And the best way to keep them on your side is to follow three cardinal rules:

- **Be organized**
- **Be clear in your direction**
- **Be open to their contributions**

THE PAPERCUT - SOUNDS PAINFUL BUT IT WILL SAVE YOUR LIFE.

To accomplish the first two of these three rules—being organized and giving clear direction--you want to create an invaluable document called the *papercut*. Just like it sounds, it is a carefully crafted road map that leads your editor to exactly which lines from your interview you want her to use. Preparing a papercut makes your editor's job easier, helps you get more familiar with your material and saves you money. Without it, your editor would need to screen every minute of your interview(s) and pick her favorite bites, beats, sections--everything. Editors are great at this, and if you have the budget, ask them to show you their own version of a first cut. But if time or money are an issue, the papercut is the way to go.

A papercut works like a script. It not only provides exact lines from your interview but it dictates the rhythm of your final piece. Here's a sample from a DVD bonus feature I created for the film *Firehouse Dog*. I wanted this section about casting the lead canine to be punchy and fun, so this is what I gave my editor:

MIKE WERB: We didn't want a dog that people had really seen before.

TODD HOLLAND: Which frankly, instantly ruled out Labradors.

MW: Jack Russell Terriers were immediately out.

CLAIRE-DEE LIM: We didn't want a Dalmatian.

TH: We couldn't have a mutt--

TH: We've seen border collies do this.

MW: Basenjis

C-DL: Australian Shepherds

TH: Chihuahuas, Doodles

MW: Dachshunds

TH: Golden Doodles, Labra Doodles

MW: I was pushing for a Poodle.

[pause]

C-DL: When I heard about that, I actually had a panic attack.

MW: Nobody liked that idea but me.

This gave me the staccato rhythm I was after. Other times I let the conversation flow more smoothly and allowed my partners to speak in greater depth. Your choices are best made on the papercut and molded into the editorial process. Nothing is set in stone, but this is a dynamite way to start.

THE TRANSCRIPTION

The very first step in creating a papercut is to get hold of the raw material – the transcription from your interview. Immediately after your shoot, ask your editor to create a low-resolution QuickTime movie (.mov or .MP4) of all the raw footage with "visible source code burned-in." This means she will superimpose a running digital clock right onto the screen, usually in a corner or at the bottom so as not to obscure your partner's face. This allows you or anyone screening the footage to reference exact clips without estimating. If your interview is only a couple minutes long, this is less important, but when you have lots of footage or multiple interviews, "burn-in," as it's abbreviated, becomes crucial.

KEY TIP: KEEP A COPY OF THE QUICKTIME FOR YOURSELF.

Next send this movie to your transcriber, but keep a copy for yourself as well. You may want to verify which lines were said clearly, if your partner was scratching her nose as she spoke or any number of other items. Having a copy of the footage is the quickest way to check.

There do exist some automated transcription services, which employ voice-recognition software, but I don't recommend them at this stage of the technology. It works similar to the way "Siri" operates and is about as hilariously fallible. It's also notoriously weak on punctuation. That may sound picky but punctuation is very important in making your papercut read like natural speech. Stick with human transcription services for now. For recommendations, please go to GoodQuestionTheBook.com.

Tell your transcriber exactly what you want including…

- **When you need the transcription back** - If it's a rush, make sure to mention it.
- **Double-space the document** - This makes it much easier to read and take notes.
- **Don't include every, *uh*, *um* & *y'know*** - Or it becomes unreadable.
- **Omit your questions and only transcribe the answers** - This cuts the size of your transcription in half and is my usual instruction, though not always.
- **Add time code internally ever thirty seconds or so** - If your partner speaks for a long time, you'll want something like this:

  RICHARD GERE - 03:03:49:23 When I saw the test of her I said, wow, this girl is just beautiful but she's eighteen years old. 03:04:28:19 But she was kind of timeless and the four of us fit together just instinctively, 03:04:58:09 So it's a kind of unconscious agreement that actors make with each other.

- **Anything else that is specific to your project** - You might need descriptions of the b-roll you shot, wardrobe notes or if you stepped on your partner's line. Whatever you can think of, tell the transcriber in advance.
- **Get each transcription as it's completed** – If you are working with multiple interviews, ask for the transcriptions as soon as each one is done. If you don't, she may deliver all of them at once and cause an unnecessary delay.

- **KEY TIP: Indicate pauses with dashes (--) instead of ellipses (…)** - Some transcribers designate a pause or a change of the subject with an ellipse, thus:

    HARRY CONNICK, JR.: And so…I see her true colors right away. She isn't…she doesn't realize that she has a big meeting the next morning.

There's nothing wrong with this except that it conflicts with one of my own practices. I use ellipses in a papercut to shorten a line or indicate that I've pulled something from another source. Ask your transcriber to use dashes instead of ellipses so there's no confusion.

On average, it takes about five times the length of the raw material to type it up, so assume a fifteen-minute interview will take over an hour to transcribe. Consequently, give your transcriber at least one business day for three thirty-minute interviews.

CHAPTER FOURTEEN

THE THREE-DOCUMENT SYSTEM

After much trial and error I've discovered an efficient process with which to create, organize and revise a papercut. I call it the Three-Document System (3DS). It streamlines the process, arranges your favorite lines in one place, creates a reliable set of back-ups in another, and culls all the junk. Try it and adapt it to your needs.

To get started, open the transcription you're working with and re-save it with a unique name. I use [ProjectName]_TRANSC_[person], which looks like this in real life:

GameOfThrones_TRANSC_P.Dinklage

When you have multiple interviews, this helps organize them as your computer will self-sort them alphabetically. If you have only one interview, it's still a good idea to be consistent.

Then, create three new documents:

1. [ProjectName]_WKSHT_v1
2. [ProjectName]_PAPERCUT_v1
3. [ProjectName]_SCRAPS_v1

KEY TIP: COLOR-CODE IT.

If you are working with more than one interview, I suggest you color code your transcriptions before you start your papercut. Pick a unique color for each speaker and change the font of that entire document. If you decide to do it later, it's time consuming and error-prone. For clarity include a legend at the top of your papercut like this:

LEGEND - WALK THE LINE

JOAQUIN PHOENIX (Johnny) - RED

REESE WITHERSPOON (June) – PINK

TYLER HILTON (Elvis)– BLUE

JAMES KEACH (Producer) - BROWN

CATHY CONRAD (Producer) - GREEN

STEP ONE - COMPILE YOUR WORKSHEET

Read through the transcription slowly. Some moments will jump out at you as perfect, while others might not look as good on paper as you remember from your interview. Don't worry about this. You're in a different headspace now than you were in the room, and you have a different goal. Instead of making sure your partner is comfortable and engaged, you're now trying to tell a compelling story.

Highlight and underline each phrase that you think *even might* work. If you underline half the document, that's fine, even if you're repeating yourself. You'll edit ruthlessly later but, for now, give yourself plenty to work with.

After underlining a phrase, copy and paste it to your WK-SHT doc. You'll be adding to this doc over and over again so leave a space between each addition. Then, rinse and repeat until you finish the transcription and your WKSHT is full of *selects*. Next:

1. **Reformat the transcription to single space.**

2 **Save your new doc to your Transcriptions folder with an X in front of the name:**

   xGameOfThrones_TRANSC_P.Dinklage

   This groups all your finished interviews together, and indicates what you still have to work on.

3. **Highlight the entire single space transcription and *copy* it to the bottom of your PAPERCUT**—Create a section at the bottom of your PAPERCUT under a heading: COMPLETE TRANSCRIPTIONS. This will give you a running inventory of all the transcriptions in one place making it simple to scan for a line or a phrase later.

If you only have one interview, you're ready to move on to the next step. If you have multiple interviews, repeat this process until you've gone through all your interviews.

STEP TWO – THE JIGSAW PUZZLE

This is where the fun begins. Read through your selects and start putting them in order on your PAPERCUT. Your WKSHT will naturally contain a lot of junk and repetition all shuffled together. That's fine; you may need some of this material later. Not every take is going to be perfect and you'll be glad you have some *safeties*.

Start to build a narrative. Some material will present itself suggesting a structure. Other stuff will make you wonder what you were thinking. When you find a line you like, *remove* it from your WKSHT and add it to your PAPERCUT. This will build a roadmap for the editor as well as whittle down your selects.

Now find a flow. Look for whole beats that work on their own: sections where your partner talked about something in detail with a beginning, middle and end. These chunks can be moved around in large sections to give shape to your piece.

If you're unsure about the flow, read the section out loud. Put yourself in the mind of the viewer as you work. If something feels disjointed or boring, it is. If something isn't working at the end, the culprit is often at the beginning. When it clicks you'll know it.

Pay particular attention to getting the top and tail of your PAPERCUT. These are "load-bearing" sound bites, so you want to nail them. Did you find two favorite possible opening lines? Try one as a *closer*, then swap them around to see which works best. Be bold; this is where you can try anything!

STEP THREE – DON'T TOSS OUT THE SCRAPS

As you rearrange your selects onto the PAPERCUT, you're going to disqualify some gems as well as some junk. Losing some of your favorite material is a requisite of any creative endeavor, but the 3DS offers you a failsafe. After selecting your A-material, save everything else as a back-up; that's where SCRAPS comes in. Cut and paste the lines you *won't* be using to your SCRAPS doc. The ultimate goal is to delete everything from your WKSHT doc. All your favorites should end up in your PAPERCUT, all the crap in SCRAPS, and WKSHT will be retired, devoid of information. That's the beauty of the 3DS: it becomes a 2DS with all the pieces you want in one place, and the dross in another.

SCRAPS is also handy if the client asks, "Don't you have anything better?" It happens. You've obviously chosen your favorite bites, but you might need to present some alternates. Since it can create tension to send your client the entire transcription, show her that you've kept a list of second choices and pull some back-ups from ol' Scrappy.

KEY TIP: ONE PAGE = THREE MINUTES

When you've completed your papercut, make sure to consider the length of your final spot. A general rule is that one page of single-spaced papercut works out to approximately three minutes of runtime.

YOUR SECRET WEAPON: THE FRANKENBITE

If you hit a dead end, or you just need one more word or phrase that wasn't *exactly* said by your partner, cautiously avail yourself of the monstrously powerful *Frankenbite*. But beware.

Editors fear frankenbites and good producers avoid them in all but drastic cases. If not carefully crafted, they can make your partner sound like she's reading an audio ransom note. In the right circumstances, however, the frankenbite will save your butt! Treat it like fire: a boon to mankind, but don't let it get away from you.

Like Frankenstein's Monster--an amalgam of body parts re-assembled to form a ungainly creature--a frankenbite is a sound bite that has been edited together from different parts of your interview to sound like a new, cohesive thought. You can slice and dice all kinds of disparate elements from your interview to make a new line, but make sure of two things: that your partner still sounds like a human being, and that you honor what she meant. The first point is obvious. So is the second, for that matter, but it's easier to ignore. It's acceptable to create a frankenbite that clarifies or shortens something. Just don't use this technique to invent content.

As I mentioned in the instructions to your transcriber, indicate a frankenbite on your papercut with ellipses (...). If you don't, your editor will assume that the line in your PAPERCUT is in the interview verbatim and go crazy looking for something that doesn't exist. These three little dots tell her you've cobbled together a new line from different places.

Also as you can imagine, compiling random words from your interview presents a fair chance for an audio train wreck. Sometimes it flies, and sometimes it sounds awful. Here are some guidelines to improve your odds:

- **Choose phrases rather than individual words whenever possible**
- **Listen to the line as soon as it's assembled to make sure it sounds human**

- Make sure you have cutaways to cover the video (more about this below)
- Never change the spirit of what your partner is saying (bears repeating)

The advantages to frankenbites are that they solve storytelling problems, save run time and even address some notes that are otherwise impossible. For example, if your client asks, "Did she ever say her co-star's name and the title together?" The answer may be no, but it wouldn't be hard to make it *yes* if you have the right elements. It's perfectly fine to put two thoughts together to sound like one, or edit out the odd "um…uh, y'know…" to clean it up. For example, this stays within the guardrails:

> KIEFER SUTHERLAND: This year… 24… is set in London, England and it's the first time we've actually… shot fully on location.

Final warning: only use the awesome power of the frankenbite when you must. Making one work requires a skilled editor to finesse the audio and hide the seams. A red flag is when you're papercut starts looking like:

> He's…a great …cinematographer…and…we heard …so much …buzz about…him.

If you have to chop up this many words to make your point, make a different point.

KEY TIP: SEND THE PAPERCUT TO YOUR CLIENT FOR PRE-APPROVAL.

Save time and money by sharing your papercut with your client. Best-case scenario: she looks it over and gives you feedback before you even get into the edit bay. The first time I did this, my client was so amazed that she never gave me another note. And even if there are a ton of notes, it's better to address them on paper before you've spent time and money in the bay.

A slightly devious colleague of mine often includes what he calls "fire hydrant lines" in his papercut to the client. These are bites that he knows will probably get cut. He feels that some clients need to mark their territory, and this gives them "something to pee on." This tactic can divert attention away from other sections you want to protect, but be careful. Your client might like the fire hydrant lines and you'll end up with junk you never wanted!

TO TIME CODE OR NOT TO TIME CODE

If you have the time or you're feeling generous, add time code to each line of your PAPERCUT. This helps your editor find the bites quickly and easily. I only recommend this, however, if you are working with a short PAPERCUT--one page or so. After that it becomes an onerous job. Any frankenbites you use, for example, come from multiple places so you'll need to time code every section of that monster. It could end up looking like this:

> **DAN POVENMIRE: 02:32:45** He goes through Vader's trash... **02:34:25:00** because... **01:02:27:19** he wants to be ...**02:27:42:05** an evil Jedi. But... **02:31:02:08** Ferb gets hit with the Sith-inator.

The good news is there's a way around this and I don't mean the diabolical, "Hey, just leave it to your editor to figure out" either. I mean: leave it to your editor's computer!

KEY TIP: LET THE COMPUTER FIND THE BITES.

If the following sounds a little too technical, simply run it by your editor. Most are self-described Gear Heads and love learning the latest technology if they don't know it already.

Avid Media Composer, commonly referred to as simply The Avid, offers a plug-in (an additional piece of software) called PhraseFind, and it's bloody magic. It is powered by Nexidia's phonetic recognition software to scan media and find the sound bites that you're after. This is primarily for un-transcribed interviews and works best when searching for specific phrases. Since it's phonetic, it takes a little while to get the hang of it.

A similar but more efficient plug-in for our purposes is called ScriptSync. This uses Nexidia's phonetic recognition engine to 'attach' footage directly to your transcription. Your editor inputs the document, and can then keyword-search the document inside Media Composer. She can click on a sentence or phrase she wants, and the computer will jump to the exact point in the footage. It works great, and it's a whole lot faster than typing in time codes. You can now create any number of unholy frankenbites, pulling individual words from all over your interview and cramming them together in any order you want. But, you know, don't.

CHAPTER FIFTEEN

EDITING YOUR INTERVIEW

U p to now, you've been preparing your project to hand over to an editor. If you've followed the steps I've suggested, she will be able to hit the ground running. In this chapter I won't try and cover everything there is to know about working with post-production professionals. Instead, I will continue to concentrate on the specific tools you need to craft this unique breed of creative: the Interview.

CLOSE YOUR EYES FOR THE RADIO CUT

No matter what the material, you're telling a story with a beginning, middle and end. Covering it with images, graphics and b-roll will support that story, but the lion's share of your project is going to be the content of your interview. The papercut will take you a long way down that road. Now it's time for your editor to assemble it into something called the *radio cut*.

The radio cut is a compilation based on your papercut, exactly as you wrote it without any fixes, suggestions, cut-aways or b-roll. It's intentionally raw and looks jumpy, disjointed and a little ridiculous (especially the frankenbites). That's OK. You're not supposed to actually watch it! You only want to pay attention to the *audio* so, if you can possibly control yourself, play it with your eyes closed. Listen to the dialogue as if you were hearing it on the radio. When you do, you will immediately notice the status of a number of issues:

- How long is the piece / how long should it be?
- Which lines sound perfect/which looked better on paper?
- Are your frankenbites seamless sentences/or ear-jarring monstrosities?
- Are the beats in the right/or wrong order?
- Are your first & last lines doing the heavy lifting?

Give this radio cut your complete attention and make as many revisions to your PAPERCUT as necessary. Listen to multiple radio cuts and revise the PAPERCUT until the audio sounds perfect. Your editor will love this because you're taking care of issues before she spends time adding b-roll, cleaning up the ums and uhs, color correcting, etc. Once the audio works, the video tends to fall into place, so if you can get your radio cut to really *sing*, the rest will be soooo much easier.

KEY TIP: DON'T SEND THE RADIO CUT TO YOUR CLIENT.

One important caveat to this step: I do not recommend sending a copy of *this* to your client. No matter how savvy she is, how many spots she's cut herself or how familiar with rough-cuts, clients tend to freak out at spots that look this unpolished. It needs so much work that you don't want notes at this stage. The radio cut is a work-in-progress for your ears only. Do yourself a favor and don't even let her know you're taking this intermediate step.

OPEN YOUR EYES FOR B-ROLL & CUT-AWAYS

Once you have the radio cut in good shape, you're ready to perfect the video. This is largely the purview of your editor so, unless you have specific suggestions, let her take a pass at this on her own. Keep in mind that wherever you've created franken-bites, your partner's head is going to jump all over the screen. You can only get away with this, therefore, if you have something to cut away to while your partner is pretending to say the line you invented. If you've chosen words that fit together naturally, and you've provided some room tone for your editor to incorporate, you should get away with it--as long as you have something to cover the video.

B-roll is anything other than footage of your partner. You can also use *clips* if available – the difference being that clips have audio, and b-roll does not. Whatever you call it, supply your editor with as much as possible to work with. This can be any additional shoot footage that relates to the topic. Graphics work nicely when appropriate. Stills are great, but video is better. If you need assets from your client, request the material as early as possible.

Another great solution is cutting to your second angle if you had the luxury of a two-camera shoot. This works perfectly in the middle of a single line, but you can only do it once, or it starts to look erratic. The best solution is variety. Use all the elements you have and your interview will feel fresh and lively, and not like a bunch of talking heads.

Conversely, try and stay on your partner's face whenever possible. She is the focus of your piece so don't feel like you need to hide her with fancy editing for no reason. Cut-aways are great but they should augment your interview, not replace it.

FINISHING THE EDIT – HAVE A BLAST!

There are dozens of lessons and tips I've learned about working with editors, and I could talk about them all day, but this book is about interviews, and we've come to the end of that process. The only thing left is for me to remind you that the person you interviewed is going to see this. Your partner put herself on the line when she agreed to sit down in front of a camera. Show her your gratitude by making her look and sound great.

CHECKLIST: EDITING YOUR INTERVIEW

PREPPING THE EDITOR / BUILDING YOUR PAPERCUT

- √ Have your editor create a low-res video with burned-in visible source time-code
- √ Send your transcriber the video of your interview (Keep a copy for yourself)
- √ Give your transcriber detailed instructions
- √ Find out when to expect the transcriptions back

THE 3DS

- √ After receiving the transcriptions, color code each one
- √ Underline your favorite bites
- √ <u>Copy</u> and paste each bite you like to your WKSHT
- √ Save the transcription and paste a copy to the bottom of your PAPERCUT
- √ Read the WKSHT for favorite bites
- √ <u>Cut</u> and paste sections to your PAPERCUT and organize
- √ <u>Cut</u> and paste the stuff you don't need to SCRAPS
- √ When you're done, WKSHT will be blank

SPECIFIC LINES

- √ Beware the Frankenbite, then use as necessary
- √ Double check your first and last lines against the QT

- √ Time code your papercut if it's short (or leave it to the Avid if it's long)
- √ Check your timing: 1 page of text = 3 minutes of air time
- √ Send this final papercut to your client for approval
- √ When approved, give the papercut to your editor

IN THE EDIT BAY

- √ Listen to the Radio Cut with your eyes closed
- √ Revise the radio cut until the audio is perfect (but <u>don't</u> share with client)
- √ Provide B-roll to your editor for cut-aways and coverage
- √ Let your editor work her magic

CHAPTER SIXTEEN

THE MARTINI SHOT

Congratulations – you've made it to the *martini shot*, the last shot of the day–or in this case, the last chapter.[13] By reading this book, you've taken some major steps toward perfecting a skill that never goes out of style. What could be more fun, or more impressive, than working with top celebrities and delving into the nuts and bolts of what they do for a living? If you use my suggestions and Key Tips, you'll not only hold your own in any interview situation, but you'll have a great time doing it! A wise friend of mine rates parties by whether she has one great conversation with someone interesting during the night. You'll be doing that for a living.

---

[13] Not to be confused with the less well-known Abby Singer Shot, named for a production manager who announced the second-to-last shot of the day so his crew could start wrapping gear early.

In this ever-changing media landscape, you might wonder if junket interviews will be around much longer. Or will they go the way of the dodo, and all this preparation is for naught? I have some encouraging input on the subject from a very credible source. Michelle Marks, Senior Vice President of Theatrical Marketing for 20th Century Fox said this:

> Junket questions will always be relevant because viewers want to hear from the movie stars themselves. They love the glamour and the chemistry. Behind-the-scenes is a fantasy, and there's always some level of escapism seeing the movie star engaging with the public.

Technology will change, but curiosity remains a constant. The skill you're mastering is going to be valuable for as long as there is human interaction, and that's not going anywhere.

Of course, there is more than one way to skin a cat, as the gruesome saying goes. There are as many different interview techniques as there are people conducting them. My way works for me, and I hope some of the tips I've suggested will help you, too. Your individual style is going to grow from your own personality and experience. You will develop your own specialties and tricks as soon as you get into the arena. I know a producer who swears by the *subterfuge* technique where he pretends he's not rolling yet (he is), and just tells his partner he wants to "get to know her" before they start. He asks all his questions without ever looking at his notes, then, once he's got what he needs, declares, "…and you're done! I was kidding, we were rolling the whole time." That works great, sometimes. Other producers present themselves as investigative journalists with reams of research on their lap to intimidate their partners into telling the truth. This isn't my style, but maybe it's yours. Find out what works best for you. Be creative, but be careful.

LAST KEY TIP: HAVE SOMEONE INTERVIEW YOU.

You will never really understand the feeling of psychic vulnerability that your partner experiences until you've looked down the barrel of a camera personally. Do yourself a favor and put yourself in her shoes at least once. Find out if you suffer from red light fever by getting someone to interview you on-camera. This exercise will allow you to empathize with what your partner is up against, and help you appreciate her perspective. You are asking her to open up and expose her innermost feelings, while surrounded by cameras, lights, microphones and a partner she's never laid eyes on before. It's both a skill and an act of courage, which you'll appreciate better when you've been on the business end of a camera yourself.

AFTERGLOW

Don't be surprised if you experience a feeling of elation, and maybe a little exhaustion after your interview. It's as if you have just finished a performance yourself; because you have. You allowed an artist to share unique insights by creating a safe space where she could open up in a meaningful way. That's no small achievement. I often feel melancholy as I say goodbye to my partner. If you give your complete attention to someone with an encouraging and supportive attitude, you'll be amazed at the emotions it brings up.

In the future, I hope you will use this book for your reference and support. I've tried to make each section specific so that you can find what you're looking for when you need a refresher. What might seem outside your expertise today could come in handy tomorrow. As I mentioned at the top, when I was starting out I couldn't find a book that laid out the mechanics of conducting great celebrity interviews. I hope this book supplies you with that kind of toolbox. When you have a moment, please let me know your thoughts at GoodQuestionTheBook.com, and follow me on Instagram & FaceBook for updates and valuable assets to make sure your future projects run smoothly.

Finally, take some advice from some of the best actors in the field, many of whom I hope you'll meet in the future. Do your preparation carefully, study your questions until you've got them down cold, then *forget it* and have fun! You can't ask for a better roadmap to success.

Now break a leg.

ACKNOWLEDGEMENTS

My heartfelt appreciation goes out to all those who have encouraged me in this endeavor, read my early writings and offered me their thoughts on the project. I am also greatly obliged to those who shared with me their own experiences to augment my perspective. They are, in no particular order: editor/dramaturge extraordinaire (and dear friend) Lana Griffin; Michelle Marks at Fox for her invaluable details on the ever-changing dynamics of press junkets; Master Mixer Tony Friedman of Outpost Mixing for his sound advice; Steven Wacks for his technical and spiritual leadership; Alicia Biggs for keeping me honest on-set and off, rock star line producer Alex Hamilton; Greg Huson, Dave Bogosian and the killer post professionals at Secret Headquarters; the incomparably creative Clark Fairfield; show runner and counselor in all things Carol Barbee, Kelley Nichols at Warner Bros. International for the *Juay De Rito* story and Craig Adams at The CW for the Charlize Theron story.

I also greatly appreciate the many clients, colleagues and friends who have hired or counseled me to do what I love:

ACKNOWLEDGEMENTS

Adam Goodwin, Adam Gross, Adam Lewinson, Andy Lueders, Alicia Katz, Anne Sweeney, Bethany Rooney, Billy Hall, Carlos Lacámara, Chris McKenna, Christian White, Chuck Saftler, Craig Peralta, David Ambroz, David Chustz, David Pearlman, Denny Tu, Diane Robina, Eric Covert, Eric Shiu, Gary Marsh, Geoffrey Carignan, Heather Rim, Heather Roymans, Jeff Strong, Jessie Marcus, Josh Shurtleff, Kevin Lahr, Kim Adelman, Lauren Cassidy, Makenzie Scott, Mary Clare Baquet, Maureen Timpa, Monica Hinden, Naomi Bandison, Noah Edelson, Patricia Tong, Paul Alan Smith, Rachael Reitman, Rasheda Donner, Richard Loomis, Rick Clifton, Rick Reebenacker, Rick Scott, Sean Moore, Thomas Ruffner, Tiffany Iino, Valerie Roper-Carillo, Xav Dubois and so many others too numerous to name.

AND A SPECIAL THANKS TO THOSE WITH WHOM I'VE PARTNERED:

Aaron Eckhart	Breanna Yde
Adam Sandler	Brad Pitt
Amy McAdams	Bryan Cranston
Anna Faris	Carey Mulligan
Arnold Schwarzenegger	Cee-Lo Green
Ashley Judd	Charlie Hunnam
Barbara Hershey	Chris Evans
Bella Thorne	Chris Pine
Ben Affleck	Chris Rock
Beyoncé	Claire Danes
Betty White	Curb Your Enthusiasm Cast

Danny Boyle
Danny DeVito
David Duchovny
Denzel Washington
Dermot Mulroney
Diane Keaton
Diane Lane
Dove Cameron
Ed Helms
Eddie Izzard
Ellen Page
Eugene Levy
Forest Whitaker
Frank Langella
George Clooney
Cast & Creators of GLEE
Halle Berry
Harry Conick, Jr.
Henry Winkler
Hugh Jackman
Ioan Gruffudd
Jack Black
James Cameron

Jamie Lee Curtis
Jane Fonda
Joaquin Phoenix
Jesse James
Jason Bateman
Jennifer Aniston
Jennifer Garner
Jennifer Love Hewitt
Jennifer Morrison
Jessica Alba
Jim Carrey
Joel Kinnaman
Jon Voight
Joseph Gordon-Levitt
Josh Brolin
Josh Duhamel
Josh Gad
Josh Lucas
Julia Louis-Dreyfus
Julia Stiles
Julianne Moore
Justin Timberlake
Kane Hodder

ACKNOWLEDGEMENTS

Katey Sagal
Katherine Heigl
Keanu Reeves
Kelsey Grammer
Kerry Washington
Kevin Hart
Kirk Douglas
Kristin Bell
Leonardo DiCaprio
Luke Wilson
Matthew Broderick
Mark Wahlberg
Martin Short
Meg Ryan
Megan Fox
Mel Gibson
Marla Frazee
Michael Douglas
Michelle Monaghan
Minnie Driver
Mireille Enos
Mythbusters: Jamie Hyneman & Adam Savage

Natalie Portman
Noomi Rapace
Oliver Stone
Orlando Bloom
Owen Wilson
Queen Latifah
Rachel McAdams
Redfoo/Barry Gordy, Jr.
Reese Witherspoon
Renee Zellweger
Richard Dreyfuss
Richard Gere
Robert Wagner
Robin Williams
Robert Englund
Ron Perlman
Sacha Baron Cohen/Borat
Sarah Jessica Parker
Sean Connery
Seth Rogen
Shia LaBeouf
Sigourney Weaver
Sofia Carson

Stan Lee	Tom Hanks
Steve Carell	Tom Hardy
Steve Howey	Tom Holland
Steve Martin	Weeds Cast & Creators
Stephen Amell	William H. Macy
Stormchasers: Sean Casey & Reed Timmer	Winona Ryder
	Zendaya
Thomas Haden Church	Zooey Deschanel
Tim Allen	

ABOUT THE AUTHOR

KENNY RHODES is an Emmy-winning producer, director and President of Polaris Productions based in Southern California. A native Angeleno, Kenny received a BA in Theater from UCLA as well as a number of oddly-named acting accolades (e.g. the Robert Reed Shakespeare Award). For twenty years, he earned his living performing on stage and screen, primarily in musicals. This led to an eight-year stint as the Tenor with The Foremen, a political, satirical folk quartet on Warner/Reprise Records. After the band's farewell "Circling The Drain Tour," Kenny was offered a job at FX Networks, working his way up to writer/producer. In 2005 he launched Polaris Productions. Now, with over 300 celebrity interviews under his belt, Kenny is the go-to interviewer for studios and networks alike. He currently lives in Pasadena with his wife Donna, their son Jerome, two dogs and an over-abundant garden. Good Question! is his first book.

www.ingramcontent.com/pod-product-compliance
Lightning Source LLC
Chambersburg PA
CBHW070446090426
42735CB00012B/2472